EFFECTIVE COMMUNICATION IN RELATIONSHIPS & COUPLE SKILLS (2 IN 1)

33+ SKILLS, ACTIVITIES & QUESTIONS TO HELP YOU BETTER COMMUNICATE, DEEPEN YOUR CONNECTION & ENHANCE INTIMACY & PASSION IN YOUR LIFE

FAYE PALMER

© **Copyright 2021 - All rights reserved.**

The contents of this book may not be reproduced, duplicated or transmitted without direct written permission from the author.

Under no circumstances will any legal responsibility or blame be held against the publisher for any reparation, damages, or monetary loss due to the information herein, either directly or indirectly.

Legal Notice:

This book is copyright protected. This is only for personal use. You cannot amend, distribute, sell, use, quote or paraphrase any part or the content within this book without the consent of the author.

Disclaimer Notice:

Please note the information contained within this document is for educational and entertainment purposes only. Every attempt has been made to provide accurate, up to date and reliable complete information. No warranties of any kind are expressed or implied. Readers acknowledge that the author is not engaging in the rendering of legal, financial, medical or professional advice. The content of this book has been derived from various sources. Please consult a licensed professional before attempting any techniques outlined in this book.

By reading this document, the reader agrees that under no circumstances is the author responsible for any losses, direct or indirect, which are incurred as a result of the use of information contained within this document, including, but not limited to, —errors, omissions, or inaccuracies.

CONTENTS

Introduction   v

Part I
THE HOW, WHAT, WHY, WHEN, AND WHERE OF COMMUNICATING IN A RELATIONSHIP:

1. HOW: Effectively Communicating with Your Partner   3
2. WHAT: Needs and Desires   26
3. WHY: Dealing with Root Causes   43
4. WHO: Narrative Therapy in Couples' Communication   59
5. WHEN: Recognizing the Crisis Point and the Breaking Point   70
6. WHERE: Reconsidering Your Environment   81

Part II
THE HOW, WHAT, AND WHERE OF MAINTANING A STRONG RELATIONSHIP:

7. Classes Bring Couples Closer Together   93
8. Perfect Vacations for Couples   102
9. Fun activities to Keep the Relationship Fresh   113
10. Sex and Communication and How to Bring it All Together   124

Part III
THE HOW, WHAT, WHY, WHEN, AND WHERE OF COMMUNICATING IN A BREAKUP

11. The Elephants in the Room   139
12. Why, When, What, and How to End it Gracefully   151

13. The How, When, and Where of Moving on from a   172
    Breakup
14. The Hows, When, and Whys of Getting Back   185
    Together

    Conclusion   201

INTRODUCTION

Many of us are in an intimate, romantic relationship of some kind. And a lot of those relationships aren't exactly perfect. While nothing truly is, a lot of these relationship can be improved.

Miscommunication or a lack of communication is often the cause of the problem in couples' relationships. It is both symptomatic and causal of a variety of other significant, even life-threatening conditions. Lack of clear communication destroys relationships, and of all sorts; romantic, familial, friendly, and professional.

The fact is that, in this information-packed world, being able to communicate clearly is vital, crucial not only to our success but also to your happiness, even our very survival.

Yet surprisingly, better communications skills are still out of reach for millions of people all over the world. There are lots of causes, including overthinking, suppressed emotions, inappropriate displays of anger, and aggression. This can also be due to a number of conditions and disorders and even complexes.

It's vital to know what you're dealing with, why it's happening, when, and where this miscommunication happens. It's crucial to know how to communicate better and more clearly, to your friends and family and coworkers, and especially your romantic partner.

This is just the book for you! No matter where you are in the romantic cycle; between partner and determined to do better, or in the crux of a crisis moment that you're afraid your relationship may not survive. And you could be right!

We'll move quickly and thoroughly through the causes and cures for this communication breakdown and tell you just how to fix it in each and every case. We'll work through different communications techniques, discuss what the real motivations might be, deep-rooted causes, ways to recognize and deal with crisis points and breaking points, and other relationship issues. We'll take a look at when and where these points may occur and how to handle them. The book makes complex theories easy to understand, with examples and exercises to get you on the road to a better romance immediately.

We'll also give you tons of practical suggestions on how, when, and where to go to improve your relationships, a virtual handbook of romantic travel and adventure which may take you to Paris ... or to your own backyard.

We'll use journalism's classic *5 W's & an H* rule (*who, what, where, when, why,* and *how*) to take you through every stage of a relationship and show you precisely how to understand and communicate your wants and desires. We'll go through the nuts and bolts of communication at the early, middle, and crucial late stages of your relationship. We'll coach you through communication breakdowns and crises. The information contained here will give you the necessary skills to navigate a breakup and to recover from it efficiently. We'll offer tips and tricks which just may lead you right back into your ex-partner's arms, if that's what you really want.

We'll take you through various schools of psychological thought, a virtual primer in modern psychology and communication theory that will help you not only with your inner life, your intimate partnerships, but with friendships and professional relationships too.

We are dedicated to bringing the latest information to our readers to make their lives easier and better. We know everybody's life could be improved in different ways and we are happy to do all we can to guide, instruct, and encourage anybody who is willing to help themselves. We make dizzying concepts easy to understand and to apply! My own journey through life (like most people's) has had its share of communication breakdowns, on almost every level. But it was with my partners that I often had the most trouble, because those relationships are the most delicate and in a lot of ways the most important. But I've learned from my mistakes, and now you can too!

This book has innumerable exercises and techniques to help any couple communicate better. The information here has been proven to rescue failing romances, and it can do the same for you. But this book can also help you communicate better with your family, your friends, and your coworkers. It will give you a better understanding of yourself and may set you on a course of self-improvement which makes every moment of your life better, happier, and more fulfilled. This book has insights and information that will make any person more effective, more productive, and more attractive.

And I'm not the only one. Our books have helped thousands of eager and hopeful readers, and these techniques are time-tested, research-based, and can certainly help you in any number of ways. But not just you. They've helped people I know, and they help people you know. There's so much information here, so many different aspects of communication are covered, that you're certain to know somebody who could benefit from the data you're about to obtain. You may not have a God complex, but chances are you know somebody who does have one. Have a friend who's a perfectionist? Do them a favor and get them a copy. Are you a manager with workers, they should all read this and then discuss it. The tool and techniques included here will make any office or workplace run more smoothly, efficiently, and effectively. Because this book is about more than just communication, it's about relationships. Help clear up relationship issues in the office and at home! There's a lot more here than just communicating with your partner, but so many of us do have flawed relationships that this book is of value to just about anyone.

If you incorporate just one technique from this book, you could save your relationship. Using more or all of them will revolutionize your life and the lives of those around you. Because even if they don't read it, you'll be able to guide them with what you've learned, improving their lives along with your own and without them even realizing it. They'd probably prefer it that way!

Not only is this book certain to improve your life and theirs, but it's vital that you start now! The maladies this book remedies can be insidious and even deadly. Lack of clear communication is a creeping disease which can have fatal consequences. It's like a cancer that takes hold before you realize and then spreads to every other facet of your life. And it can be just as deadly, leading to depression, abuse, the consequences of ill-health, even suicide.

Don't let things go too far, don't let that cancer spread. You hold in your hands the scalpel you need, the cure for what may be slowly killing your relationship and ruining your life. Don't wait another second! Your relationship can't afford it, you can't afford it. And your friends and family may be suffering too. The sooner you help yourself, the sooner you can help them!

Don't get caught in the trap of analysis paralysis, don't overthink, don't let negative self-talk or a fixed mindset prevent you from opening up new doors in your life and your love. This book will make it all clear and it will revolutionize the way you think, feel, and behave. You've already begun your journey, and you're more than capable of taking the next steps to save yourself and your loved ones from the common traps that ruin so many lives. The next step is the first section, the first chapter, the first day of the rest of your life.

Let's get to it!

I

THE HOW, WHAT, WHY, WHEN, AND WHERE OF COMMUNICATING IN A RELATIONSHIP:

HOW TO SAY IT, WHAT YOU'RE SAYING, WHAT IT TRULY MEANS, WHO YOU REALLY ARE WHEN YOU'RE COMMUNICATING, AND THE EFFECTS OF YOUR ENVIRONMENT

1

HOW: EFFECTIVELY COMMUNICATING WITH YOUR PARTNER

WHY BETTER COMMUNICATION ISN'T JUST IMPORTANT, IT'S CRUCIAL

Experts believe that communication skills really kick in at around age two, when words are formed and associated with basic concepts. But a two-year-old's ability to communicate is matched by the depths of their desire. They have basic thoughts, almost always self-directed (*"Gimme, it's mine."*) They even refer to the two towering influences in their lives, their parents, in terms of their own wants or needs.

And that's fine for a two-year old. But we learn over time (hopefully) that the more delicate and complex interactions of adults require a more finessed way of communicating. If, for example, you go into your adult romance saying, "Gimme, it's mine," you could lose that relationship and even personal freedom.

In fact, we learn in stages, our ability to communicate developing, evolving with our experiences. Keep in mind that there are two basic mindsets among the general population; a fixed and a growth mindset. The fixed is a closed-minded view of the world, convinced that things are the way they are, people are the way they are, and these things simply don't change. The growth mindset holds that people and their circumstances can be changed over time according to experience.

Why is this important? In truth, it's important to all things in our lives and on virtually every level. Whether you are of a fixed or a growth mindset will affect every aspect of your life; personal, professional, and social.

A romantic relationship is unique among these things for a variety of reasons, the first one being fairly obvious. The physical and spiritual intimacy anybody shares with a romantic partner, by the very nature of that type of relationship, makes each person in the relationship far more vulnerable, and they invest far more in those relationships than any others. Your boss never sees you naked (hopefully) nor they you (ditto). You're not expected to lay around snuggling and sharing your intimate secrets with your coworkers, no matter how close you are. And just as you may drift away from coworkers after transfers or job changes, you're not so apt to drift away from the romance, sometimes even years after it's over. We'll discuss this later in the book, but to further make the point about commitment; people are likely to switch jobs (roughly every four years) than spouses (probably twice in your life, perhaps three).

So how we handle ourselves in our romantic relationships is especially important. It goes to the very core of who we are. There's an old saying which goes something like, you can judge a man by the way he treats his wife. It doesn't sound very #metoo, but the point remains. The way a person treats the one with whom he or she is more intimate and loving than anyone else is a good reflection and indication of how that person will treat others. If a man would beat his wife, what would he do to a total stranger?

I don't mean to simplify the concept of physical or marital abuse, of course. There's a lot more to it than that. A man may abuse his wife only because she is the only one powerless to stop him, for a variety of psychological reasons.

But it is true that the way we communicate in our relationships reflects the way we communicate in other facets of our lives. A person with a fixed mindset on one level is virtually certain to have a fixed mindset on all levels. A person who is a good listener and a measured communicator in their romantic life is almost certain to behave that way with their friends and coworkers as well. It's all intertwined. So, learning how to communicate on this level is crucial to anyone's overall success and happiness.

How do we know this is true? Statistics bare it out! Studies show that married couples are almost 9% happier than divorced or separated people. Single people reported being only 0.2% happier than divorced people. Every study shows that those who have never married die earlier than those who have been married, and much earlier than those who remain married.

So, a happy, healthy romantic relationship is no doubt in our best interests. And healthy communication is absolutely vital to any healthy romantic relationships. Another look at various studies reveals that the inability to communicate is responsible for 65% of divorces. The inability to resolve conflict leads to 45% of divorces.

The men researched in a particular study cited complaining and nagging as their top communication problem. We call that blaming or shaming. Women seemed most irked by their partner's failure to value their feelings or opinions.

There can be little doubt. Clear, healthy communication is paramount to every facet of your life, and nowhere is it more important than in your romantic relationship.

WHAT YOU MAY BE DOING WRONG

But what is it about a romantic relationship which can make clear and healthy communication so difficult? Just as healthy communication is central to strong romance, we've already seen the stats of the negative effect on unhealthy communication. But the flip side is that, while communication in these relationships is central, it can also be the most challenging, and both are related to the particulars of an intimate relationship.

As we've seen, a person is most vulnerable in a romantic relationship, and they tend to invest more in those relationships. As in many transactional situations, there's a risk-to-benefit ratio. There's more risk in a personal relationship (the risk of rejection, the risk of betrayal, a costly or painful divorce and a child or children who must bear the brunt of that divorce). There's also more reward (better physical and psychological health over a longer life, a satisfying family life, children to carry on your genes and maybe take care of you when you're old).

But being so vulnerable in the face of some of these risks can affect a person's perspective, their mindset, their behavior. Fear is a powerful motivator, and anybody can become fearful over time. With that fear, anybody may want to protect their vulnerability. If a person is afraid of infidelity, they may withdraw themselves and become physically and romantically introverted. Envisioning a betrayal, they seal themselves off from the vulnerability, which is in this case the intimacy. This, of course, can become a self-fulfilling prophecy, wherein a person is fearful of being betrayed and shuts themselves off and thereby inspires their partner toward a betrayal.

More is the pity, because a simple clear line of communication would clear this up! If one is fearful of betrayal, they're making a big assumption. Assumptions, by the way, are almost always wrong; we all know what happens when you assume. Reassurance and clarification could reverse this assumption. Misread signs could be straightened out.

Romantic relationships have their own communications issues. Over time, a romantic couple may become so complacent that they simply don't bother communicating. Long out of the courtship phase, perhaps deep into a marriage, there may be little to talk about. But anybody with a growth mindset will know that a person is likely to grow over time, to evolve with the effect of experience. So, there should always be something new to talk about, really. It just takes a new perspective and an open mind.

There's also another old saying (we'll be using a few, because they work) which goes, *familiarity breeds contempt.* After so many years of intimacy, of complacency, people can often get sick of each other, it's as simple as that. And instead of dealing with this problem as it happens, one or both may allow those feelings to fester until they become unbearable and the relation comes to a crashing and often acrimonious end. This is also avoidable. True, not every relationship is going to work out. Not every two people are compatible with one another, people do grow apart. But bad blood would never fester if one or the two were open with their feelings and knew how to communicate them in a healthy manner. Because it's not just a matter of being open with your feelings, as that can have disastrous results.

And it just happens to be another big particular challenge of communicating in an intimate or romantic relationship. One or the other may become prone to over-expressing, over-dramatizing, over-acting and over-reacting. This communication becomes haranguing, sniping, complaining, insulting, verbal abuse, and it can even lead to physical abuse in an escalating spiral of anger and uncontrolled temperament. These abuses, all of them, can go both ways. So, if you're going to be free with your communication, you must be disciplined with it, restrained, considerate of the other person's position. Too often, after a certain length of time, we may begin to feel that we've given this person enough, and now it's our time; for release, for attention, for whatever. If you want to have a fight, you'll be well-situated. If you want to have a friend or a lover or a spouse, you're probably going ninety miles an hour down a dead-end street.

One thing to consider is to keep in mind the difference between resentment and anger. Anger is more of a passing emotion, whereas resentment tends to linger. Often, when anger is not expressed, it becomes resentment. Anger is much easier to deal with, before it has had a chance to grow and fester. So, if you can know the difference, you can recognize each and deal with them in different ways. Anger is less destructive and can be dealt with more quickly, resentment takes more time.

Those in a romantic relationships face other particular challenges to communication as well. Research indicates that the most common source of conflict among married couples is money. A lot of failed relationships are due to arguments about money, because money has its own particular challenges when it comes to communication, especially in intimate relationships.

In America, as in a lot of countries all over the world, we are defined by our success or our failure. How many conversations get rolling with, *"So, what do you do?"* In the 1980s and beyond, when greed was good, success became even more vital to a person's self-worth, especially for men. It was a measure of his potency, of his vigor, of his strength, a sign that he was an alpha male. This all fell into the biological mandate of procreation and what the human psyche has been both trained and created to seek, desire, and do. Remember that women have only been in the American workforce for a few generations. But men have a nearly 10-000-year-long tradition of proving their worth to breed, and doing this by dominating their environment; the prairie, the Pacific and other theaters of battle, even the boardroom or the suburban block. The pressure for men to succeed is immense.

For years, this had been an upward spiral. Every generation had done better than the generation before it. That did little to alleviate the pressure, of course. But when the current generation turned out to be the first not to do as well as the previous generation, things took a turn. Jobs were harder to find, and the so-called *great recession* of 2007-2009 hit, pressure to succeed became pressure to survive.

After a historic recovery, things have taken a downward economic turn again. People are having a lot more trouble now, only increasing the pressure of money troubles. This time, the economic battering was so bad it resulted in widespread depression, substance abuse, and even suicide.

And to get back to the stats, talking about money is hard for a lot of average people even under the best of circumstances. It speaks to the center of how we see ourselves. Many of us men by a simple historical fact, though increasingly few by a simple contemporary fact. We're all suffering, prone to feelings of failure and an inability to survive. It can trigger feelings of having failed one's parents, dropped the ball on the entire country.

Economic pressures are often unrelenting. No matter how understanding and sympathetic, supportive, and loving any two people are, that won't pay the rent. It won't put food on the table or pay the car insurance bill. Those things hover over the heads of countless couples, married or not, and it can be crippling.

The ways it shut down clear, healthy communication shouldn't be unfamiliar. Tempers flare and self-control erupts into irrevocable outbursts, or fear and shame create great lulls of communication breakdown until a clear line can no longer be re-established.

These money worries resonate in even deeper ways. Think of the fixed or the growth mindset. Almost nowhere does this resonate louder than in terms of our private economies, except perhaps our romantic lives overall. But since we're looking at an even more central aspect of our lives, let's parcel this out.

First, why is money more central than love? What kind of monster would write such a thing? Is this Gordon Gecko himself? Well, I don't mean to put it that way. But our success or failure is often seen as a reflection of something within ourselves. The rugged American individual so deeply engrained in our minds, from Davy Crockett to Ronald Reagan, that we see ourselves as the stewards of the American dream. It's something we do or fail to do on our own, according to many. It's a notion which lends itself to a fixed or a growth mindset.

A fixed mindset is likely to see things which happen in his or her life to be a reflection of themselves and to be a measure of their worth. A growth mindset is more apt to focus on the circumstance and their best efforts as they relate to the circumstance. A growth mindset is more apt to be self-forgiving, because the growth mindset doesn't let the circumstance, a success or failure, reflect on the value of the person.

But both mindsets may embrace the individualistic way of doing things. It's not to say that anybody with a growth mindset must necessarily be a team-player. Some people interact well with others and find inspiration there. Others thrive on privacy and fewer distractions. It has a lot to do with whether a person is a *manager,* whose job puts them naturally into interaction with others, or a *maker,* who's job requirements generally include long hours alone. A team-playing manager might be a growth-minded person, ready to focus on the result and not the individual commitment, but they may still be fixed in their methods, trained by experience to manage chaos with a stricter sense of control. You'd likely be hard-pressed to convince a person like this that their methods are wrong, because they might not be!

Either way, you could be growth-minded or fixed-minded and still be either a manager or a maker; you still may have money troubles you don't feel comfortable with. Because a growth-minded person can be optimistic about the future but still not know how to deal with the present. The fixed-minded man or woman is likely to believe that things will never really change. This person may be less likely to advance, but they also have more stable finances.

This brings us back to my Gordon Gecko impression. We see here how central the concept of success is to how we identify ourselves, regardless of our mindset or the state of the economy. We use the phrase self-made man for a reason, and it's the American ideal.

But any romance necessarily involves a second person. It's about the other person's points of view, opinions, tastes, foibles, follies, goals, and regrets. A relationship is not found at the core of either of the individuals, but in the center of the space between them. It's a different balance of gravity. Surely, the one affects the other, but they're not the same.

And since we've seen the crippling effects of money troubles on romance, that's something to be particular careful of. We'll talk more about this later in the book too, but for now just keep it in mind! (Really, we'll be coming back to all these ideas as we work our way through the book, so don't skip over anything, you may only have to go back.)

KEYS TO CLEARER COMMUNICATION

It all seems like a lot to digest. It seems that, in order to better communicate with others, we have to get into closer touch with ourselves. That's very true, actually. We've already touched on a fixed mindset or a growth mindset. Which are you? Take a moment to think about it? Do you have a defeatist point of view, ready to anticipate a pattern of events to repeat no matter what external forces occur? Do your failures inspire you to try again, to try even harder, even knowing failure may yet be the result? You may never have given that any thought at all, but maybe it's about time you did.

And even if you're a fixed-mindset person, you don't have to stay fixed about it. Face it; you can't control everything; you can't be responsible for everything. Every success is likely to be the result of at least a few people, even if they were only your personal heroes, teachers, or mentors. So, every failure is likewise not your fault. Failures lead to successes, they're part of the process. Realize that the process can yet change the final outcome, that nothing is set in stone. That's about all you have to do.

But if you're a fixed mindset person and you want to remain that way, that's okay too. There are other ways, but as a fixed-mindset person you can at least make sure you always put away money, the same amount every month if possible. Stick to the systems which serve you; pay your taxes on time, always tell the truth.

And this is your viewpoint, know it going into the realm of intimacy and communication. If you have your ways and they're set in stone, start off by finding somebody who understands and accepts, and even embraces it. Or you might find a partner with the same rules, also set in stone. Good. Two fixed mindsets probably make a good match.

If you're a growth-minded person, you may want to avoid a fixed-minded person, or you may not. Perhaps opposites attract. But knowing what kind of person they are, and what kind of person you are, will make all the difference in whether you can communicate successfully.

Knowledge is power, after all.

There are other aspects of the individual, which should be examined when looking at communication in romantic relationships. Because the nature of intimacy and a shared life is so widespread, it touches on every aspect of ourselves and each other. Are you extroverted, on the go, a manager type? If so and your partner is too, you might actually clash, each trying to outmanage the other. Two workers may become simply a pair of introverts and fail to make a connection at all.

The way we deal with different types is different, and it's nowhere as important as in a romantic relationship. We have a much greater effect on each other than we do on most others. If you're a manager type and your worker partner are symbiotic, that's great. But the two styles may clash. Too much management may further isolate the worker-minded partner. So, understand that you communicate in a certain way and your partner in a different way. Some people are more naturally high energy, others more reserved. This can inspire, or it can annoy. Be conscious of how this may affect them.

When communicating, always keep the other person in mind above yourself. Your reactions will be easier to manage than theirs.

This is the essence of diplomacy, with will serve you well in every facet of your life. It's always the first line in every military conflict, and the first rule of diplomacy is to resolve conflicts while avoiding war. It may sound simple, but it's commonly forgotten and over overlooked. Because while sometimes a disagreement many resolve problems and strengthen a friendship, the basic fact is that we're very often not looking for a friendship, we're just looking for a fight. We may be a bit drunk or a bit fed up, but we go into the conflict seeing it as a war waiting to happen, and it almost certainly will. Too rarely do people engage with an attitude that they are entering a mission of diplomacy, not a fight at all. If they did, at least some of those fights could likely be avoided.

And how do you incorporate diplomacy into your romantic communication? Let's take a closer look.

First of all, select a time and place with privacy. Nobody should be nearby to hear it, or what is said may embarrass one or both parties. That third person maybe drawn into a conflict where they have no part. And it's crazy rude to argue in front of another person. Ever see a bickering couple at a cocktail party, maybe two drunken lovers having a fight in the middle of the frat party. Yeah, so just don't do that.

Start with what's working. Don't just tear into your list of grievances. Things can only go downward from there. But remind your partner about what's working in your relationship, what you treasure about your partner, the fond memories you have and the things you look forward to. It'll soften what's coming next and take the edge off any potential combativeness.

Remind your partner that you love them and like them and that all you want is for you both to be as happy together as you can be. That *is* the way you feel, right? If not, rethink the whole conversation.

Ask questions. It's often said that the best conversationalist in the world only talks about one thing … you. You don't want to go on and on about your angers, your needs, your judgements. That will only lead your partner to demand that it be time for their angers, needs, and judgements. That's where diplomacy often ends. And there are times when you have to represent yourself and should take the focus of the other, we'll get to them soon enough. But for now, if you're going to talk about the other person, do it in questions. Don't tell them their feelings are wrong, don't tell them how you think they should feel. But you could and should ask them about their feelings, express, and demonstrate a genuine interest in how they feel, why they feel the way they do, what they think they could change in order to stop feeling that way. But don't put all responsibility on them! Ask them what you might have done to make them feel the way they do, what you can do (if anything) to correct it. Engage, but do it in a rhetorical way. This way you're not making any declarative statements which might seem aggressive or insulting.

Listen actively, not passively. Don't just sit there and wait for your chance to insert your perspective or make your point. Really concentrate on what the other person is saying, to the feelings behind those words. Don't offer corrections or opinions, just listen. It's not as easy as it sounds, and it may take some experimentation. In our fast-paced world, we can hardly afford not to be proactive at all times. Meditation is an excellent exercise for becoming an active listener.

Without getting too deep into it, transcendental meditation includes sitting quietly and focusing on something other than the clamor of the world. It may be your breath, focusing on the in and out as you breathe. Some focus on a single focus point, other on a muttered mantra. The idea is to focus on only this thing. It trains you to focus and naturally makes you a better listener. Try it and see if you don't agree. It has lots of other benefits too.

Be empathetic. Briefly, sympathy is the capacity to feel badly for someone. Empathy is when you can imagine the very pain the other is feeling. Sympathy is a social norm, but empathy involves real emotional investment. So, since you're there with your intimate partner, perhaps your spouse, talking about the very things which may be plaguing that person's soul, invest some empathy. Imagine feeling what they're feeling, feel it deep down inside you. You may not be used to expressing empathy, but it is probably well within your reach. Try it by watching *Casablanca* or *Love Story* and see if you're not moved.

If you do have to speak and you have to say things about your partner which you might consider constructive (not likely to land that way), observe this rule; address behavior if you must, not the person's character. If sloppiness is a problem, keep it to that; no reason to diagnose that sloppiness as reflecting the person being lazy or stupid. Never go personal with it. Also, those things can be argued, but if the toilet seat is up, then the toilet seat is up; there's no argument to be had there.

If you must address your partner's behavior, follow it up quickly with a solution, which you should already have prepared in advance. Don't just go in with guns blazing and hope you're going to get what you want. Be prepared. Chinese warlord Sun Tzu said, roughly, that the general who prevails knows *that* he's going to prevail because he knows *how* he's going to prevail. He was a big believer in diplomacy too.

When you move from questions to declarations, keep them about yourself. Nobody has a right to tell somebody else how to think, how to feel, or how to express those feelings and thoughts, no matter how repulsive they may be. You can always walk away, and more often than not, that's what happens. But you always have the right to express how you feel. They can walk away, but you're not transgressing on anybody in telling them how you feel.

Keep in mind that you don't have the right to expect people to give you what you want if you're not ready to ask for it. You can't just expect them to read your minds. The old *you should have known* routine just doesn't fly anymore. So, buck up and prepare to stand your ground.

Be honest, no matter if you're speaking or listening. Avoid being frank or terse, certainly don't be rude. But nobody can blame you for being honest. Furthermore, it won't do either of you any good. If you're not being honest, you're not having a clear line of communication, period.

And when you make your declarations, there are certain strategies you can use. For example, you wouldn't say, "I feel that you're completely wrong!" That won't do the trick. Even, "I feel that I am completely right, and … seem to feel otherwise." You can't cheat this, and getting it right really isn't as easy as it sounds.

Try something like, "I feel that I'm not being heard," or "I feel tense, more and more," or even, "I feel that something is wrong between us." Hey, you feel how you feel. All the other person can do is say how they feel. It's a great way to de-escalate things if you can, even to prevent them from going haywire. Take responsibility for your actions, your place in the scheme of things between you, for your own feelings and emotions.

But watch out, as there's a hitch; some people hear the word feelings and they become insensate! You've suddenly become a so-called *snowflake,* as if you have no intellect at all and are acting only from emotion. But I find that most people who instantly aggress on the word feelings isn't an intellectual but a bully who is a slave to their own feelings, which they can almost never understand. Mentioning your feelings is a trigger for this kind of bullying attitude. It doesn't mean you shouldn't do it, but be prepared.

If somebody does get triggered in this way, the best thing to do is walk away. If this is your romantic partner, you might not be a good match. If you want to try to make it work, know what kind of communication just won't get through to that person and be prepared to accept it. Of course, this is symptomatic of a fixed mindset, and a fixed mindset can be changed, as we've seen. But that change almost always has to happen from within. A person with any mindset is likely to hold onto it only until they decide to change it. They'll cling to it all the more in the face of intervention from somebody else. Really, you can't change a person.

This person may also be an abuser. There are various types of abuse; physical, sexual, psychological. If you're that frustrated in a relationship, this person may be emotionally abusive. If they are withholding affection, show no remorse, are unusually controlling or blameful or disrespectful of your feelings, you're probably in an emotionally abusive relationship. I think you'd be hard-pressed to find anyone willing to suggest you try to change this person or the relationship. This person could have any number of psychological disorders, problems you can't solve, if they can be solved at all. Almost all abusive relationships must be escaped, not saved.

But if you're both sound of mind and truly interested, there are lots of ways to keep it going smoothly. Reflect on what your partner has said, rephrase it as you delve deeper. "I know you feel this way, that your voice isn't heard …" or whatever it is they said. It shows that you listened, understood, and that you've taken it in as a part of your personal responsibility.

Respond, don't react. Keep it reasonable, avoid emotion. When a person comes from an emotional place, they cannot be reasoned with. Likewise, emotion cannot really sway reason. It's about the brain and how it functions.

Our brains' prefrontal cortex controls logic and decision-making while the limbic system is where our emotions are found. When the prefrontal cortex inhibits the limbic system's emotional reactivity, we're all quite reasonable. But when emotions run eye, the prefrontal cortex loses control. But they operate on different levels, and once the imbalance is struck, it takes a while for the brain to recalibrate. But just know that, for practical purposes, an emotionally revved-up person just won't listen to reason. So, when things are too emotional, think about walking away. You won't get anything accomplished from that point forward, and you're likely to go on to do further or even irrevocable damage.

If that happens, don't ever be afraid to walk away from a conversation and don't let anyone pull you back in. Nobody has the right to demand that you do that. They can speak, but you don't have to listen.

When you *are* speaking, however, use collaborative language like *we, our, us*. It's a bonding technique, demonstrating that you are not only in it for yourself, that you have a shared goal. If you don't have the shared goal of keeping the relationship happy ... and alive ... then you've got other problems.

If you're still on an even keel but diplomacy doesn't seem to be working, there are other considerations. You've asked about your partner, you've expressed yourself, now what? Take a look at your environment. The environment has a huge effect on the psyche. Be constructive about what you each can do to improve the situation. Don't be judgmental, but there could be physical things which will affect your behavior and your feelings. Is it time for a good Spring cleaning? Maybe that activity will give you a chance to work together and get closer. It'll give you time to look over those old souvenirs you've got laying around, and that could lead to rekindling old feelings, reminding each of their love when it was at its fullest. Does one of you feel cramped or smothered? Perhaps an area set aside for private activities, like reading or journaling, can be set aside. Maybe a vacation together will reinvigorate a waning sex life or maybe a separate vacation would be good to correct too much familiarity.

Be creative, but be reasonable. If a vacation won't really help, it could actually hurt. The question is really about identifying the problem, which we'll look at soon. If your problem is a cluttered homelife, a weekend in Las Vegas won't help that. You'll still be coming home to the same problem. If you're wrestling with a gambling or drinking problem, Vegas *definitely* won't help that. And if money is your trouble, well, there's always a good ol'-fashioned Spring cleaning.

Think before you speak. This is something we should all do more often, but it's crucial when things get heated between you and your partner. And it's altogether too easy to speak too quickly, to say too much. And some things just can't be unsaid.

Some other great communication tips include keeping your voice down; voices escalate, one with the other, so keep it down and you'll keep it cool. Don't interrupt; listen quietly and respectfully and really listen, it may be your last chance. Be sober; don't have any big talks about anything important when either of you is under the influence. Be kind; no personal comments about the others' body, face, hair, mother, friends, pet, anything. Be brief and don't repeat yourself; if you didn't make your point after one or two tries, maybe the other person just isn't listening. Be aware of your body language; don't point, snarl, lean forward, thrust your chin, bite your lower lip, grit your teeth or clench your fists. These things will have an affect on your voice, which will feed an escalating spiral of uncontrollable rage. Be happy; come at the communication with a hope to make things better, not the certainty that they're about to become worse. Look at it as a mission of diplomacy.

Along these lines, make yourself comfortable. Don't stand face to face in the center of the room, that's the posture of combat. That's how boxers and swordsmen and barroom brawlers stand. But you're there as a diplomat, to prevent the fight. So, sit down, and in a comfortable way. Avoid power postures, like sitting somebody down in a chair and then sitting on the corner of the desk, looming above them. Don't sit them down while you stand. Don't sit them across a table from you, that's a confrontive position. Sit down side by side if you can, on a couch with nothing between you.

Make eye contact. This works in all kinds of communication, from legal and judicial interrogations to the psychological area. It's quite common in the corporate world, a direct power move. It shows that you're focused on the other person, that you're listening. Looking away makes you seem distracted, disinterested, or worse confused or dishonest.

But be careful with the eye contact, as it's a serious technique. Some may find it disquieting. If they fidget under your gaze, look away. And if you're angry, this is a particularly jarring technique and can even seem threatening.

Think good thoughts about your partner during these conversations and in general. I'm not saying anybody's a mind-reader, but these kinds of things manage to get through on a subconscious level.

Lastly, don't be afraid to apologize. It's really quite a simple thing, but some people just can't or won't do it. Research indicates that people who refuse to apologize include those who fear being seen as weak or fear retaliation or rejection that they won't be forgiven upon their admission. Some are perfectionists who feel this small failing will define them. If you're one of these people who feels this way, you might want to reconsider. It takes a real mature adult to apologize, especially when they are wrong. And we're all wrong a lot more than we realize.

It doesn't make you or anyone a victim to be on either side of an apology. We've seen that a person has to ask for what they want, they can't resent another person for not reading their mind. It doesn't make anyone a victim for asking for an apology either. It's a personal declaration and a pretty modest one at that. Chances are, if somebody believes they are owed an apology, they probably do deserve one. If you were perceived as being rude, let's say, and offended somebody inadvertently, then you should apologize for misspeaking or for being inadvertently offensive. If you meant to be rude, you definitely owe an apology, or if you've come to see that you transgressed, just apologize. It's a sign of strength to apologize.

Though if you're in a situation where you're constantly having to apologize, there could be a real imbalance there.

So be careful when communicating with your romantic partner, be mindful of the hidden traps, and use those helpful tricks.

2

WHAT: NEEDS AND DESIRES

This takes us on a trajectory going deeper, from ways of communicating, or the *how*, downward to the next level, the *what*. Because it's important to understand what you're expressing before you can express it clearly.

Basically, human motivation can be categorized as either a group of needs and a group of desires. Are you expressing a need or a desire? Let's take a closer look at both.

NEEDS

Needs are the things you must have to survive.

Abraham Maslow (1908-1970) created his hierarchy of needs as a five-tiered pyramid of the things the human psyche requires for a fulfilling life. It begins with the bottom level, the broadest and most basic but also the most requisite. These are the physiological needs of food, water, warmth, rest. Without these things, none of the others are necessary or even possible, because life cannot progress without those basic physiological needs.

Note here that Maslow himself admits that there's some overlap here. The safety needs may occur at the same time as the physiological, the physiological with the belonging and love needs, so they may not progress in a strictly orderly fashion and can't necessarily be dealt with in that fashion.

But in the basic model, only when the first level of needs is satisfied can one move up to the next tier, safety needs such as security, safety. This includes shelter. It's not strictly necessary, but it's the next step upward after the basic necessities. In less strenuous times, shelter would have been considered requisite, and it still is for a fulfilled psychology.

The third level up includes the belongingness and love needs, which include intimate relationships and friendships. Once these are in place, one may progress to the second level from the top, esteem needs. These include prestige and feeling of accomplishment.

Once one has worked through all four levels, in order, they may arrive at the top tier, self-actualization, which brings a person to achieving their full potential, with a balance of professional and personal successes.

And the entire hierarchy, all five tiers, can be divided into three categories. The first two, physiological and safety, are considered *basic needs*. The next two up, belongingness and love needs and esteem needs, are considered *psychological* needs. The upper tier, self-actualization, is a *self-fulfillment* need.

So, if what you're expressing is a need, which one is it? It's likely to be one of the psychological needs, but what if it's really a self-fulfillment need? Your partner can't be responsible for your self-fulfillment, but they do take some part in your belongingness and love needs, so it's fair to approach them on those grounds. Though they're both considered psychological needs, do you have esteem needs or the more basic belongingness and love needs? When you're in a relationship, it's important to know the difference. Also, keep in mind that in intimate relationships, a belongingness and love need, is as important to you as to anyone. It comes before esteem and well before self-actualization. So, know the value of what you're trying to preserve.

But there's even more to this fascinating psychological model. Because the five tiers can also be subdivided into either *deficiency needs* or *growth needs*. The first four, the basic and the psychological needs (physiological, safety, belonging and love, esteem) are considered deficiency needs. The top tier, self-realization, is a growth need (sometimes called a *being need*). And this only makes sense. If you lack the first four, you're deficient in them. Until you have all four, you're just catching up, not getting ahead. The fifth, top tier is where real growth happens, where advancement is achieved.

Now that the hierarchy of needs is clear, the waters muddy up again. Because the model has been modified for the modern era to include three more layers! A new fifth layer above the fourth, *cognitive needs*, includes understanding and knowledge, exploration and curiosity, a need for meaning and predictability. Think of the existential questions of identity and purpose. These things are generally resolved before the higher, self-fulfillment growth need of self-actualization.

A new sixth layer is just above cognitive, aesthetic needs. These include an appreciation of nature, the search for balance and form and beauty. Then comes self-actualization needs at number seven, with a new top layer, an eighth layer, above that; *transcendence needs*. These include values which go beyond the self, beyond the existential questions of personal place and identity to more transcendent notions of eternity, God, religious and spiritual matters. Experts would say that a truly fulfilled psyche would first need some self-actualization before being equipped to have any transcendental understanding, so that one goes at the top.

Of the new, eight-tier pyramid, the first four (physiological, safety, belonging and love, esteem) are considered deficiency needs and the upper four (cognitive, aesthetic, self-actualization, transcendent) are considered growth needs. The new hierarchy breaks down into the familiar three categories in more or less the same way: The first two, physiological and safety, are still considered *basic needs*. The next two up, belongingness and love needs and esteem needs, are still considered *psychological* needs. The upper four tiers, cognitive, aesthetic, self-actualization, transcendent, are all considered *self-fulfillment* needs.

So, what happens when a person reaches those growth needs and become self-actualized? Self-actualized men of history include Abraham Lincoln and Albert Einstein. But while anybody can theoretically become self-actualized, few people manage it. Maslow himself suggested that only two percent of people become self-actualized. So, let's take a look at what happens at the top of Maslow's hierarchy. This will help you gage where you and other people are in the hierarchy and that will help you identify needs and then be able to satisfy them.

This is especially crucial when dealing with intimate partners.

Are you self-actualized? If you've bought this book, you probably have an intimate relationship, that puts you at least at the third layer. If you're also imbued with sufficient self-esteem, then you're ready to progress upward and become self-actualized, if you don't consider yourself that already. Let's take a closer look at what a self-actualized person looks like.

According to Maslow's research, self-actualizers can tolerate uncertainty and have a clear and efficient perception of reality. They accept themselves for what they are. This means perfectionists and overthinkers, those with various complexes, are unlikely to achieve self-actualization because their perceptions of themselves and of reality is so skewed.

Self-actualized people tend to be spontaneous, they live in the moment and are not caught up in either the past or the future. They don't over-consider every option until no option at all is selected (sometimes called *analysis paralysis*).

Self-actualized people center on problems, not people. With a growth mindset, they know that failure does not define the person, and that their own efforts are not as important and the end result. In the case of failure, they learn from their mistakes and work onward toward the next challenge.

Maslow found that self-actualized people have a sometimes-peculiar sense of humor. They delight in what they think is funny, not in what they think others will find funny. They're not as concerned about what impressions others may have. They also tend to retain their individuality, they're not prone to cultural trends; though they're also not deliberately outrageous or rebellious.

Those who are self-actualized tend to look at life objectively rather than subjectively. They have a clearer perception than those who see the world only through their own experiences and perspectives. In this way, the self-actualized person is apt to be both sympathetic and empathetic. In a like vein, they tend to be concerned for others' welfare and for the future of humanity. They have transcendent concerns, but they also have deep appreciation of the basic life experiences. They may have their head in the stars, but their feet are firmly on the ground.

Self-actualized people tend also to be highly creative. They establish fewer relationships in life, but those relationships are more meaningful and tend to last longer. They tend to have had peak experiences, memorable heights to look back on. Yet they generally have a need for privacy and little need for holding the spotlight.

They also tend to have democratic social and political views and high ethical and moral standards. How many did you check off your list? Which ones are you lacking? You can remedy almost any shortcoming on the list. Don't consider yourself highly creative? Maybe you just haven't found your medium. Being creative doesn't strictly mean being artistic. You could be a creative problem-solver, for instance. Are you more politically conservative than liberal? That doesn't mean you can't be self-actualized. Don't let the list limit you, let it open doors you didn't know were there.

Let's make it easier. Instead of looking at the behaviors of self-actualized people, let's examine behaviors leading to a place of self-actualization. If you want to become more self-actualized, try doing what they do.

Try to experience life like a child, absorb everything and have curiosity and an open mind. Try new things and embrace new experiences. Listen to your own feelings, evaluate things and experiences based on your own perspective, not the common perception or that of some authority. Think for yourself.

Be honest and avoid fakery or game playing. Stand by your views even if you risk being unpopular. This is called integrity, the measure of effect a thing undergoes given the same external pressures. It's an aeronautic term, referring to how much a wing will bend given the same height, altitude, temperature, wind, and other external forces. If the wing reacts the same way given the same circumstances, its integrity is intact. Self-actualized people are reliable.

In the same way, self-actualized people take responsibility for what they do and say, and they work hard to do and say the right things, things they're prepared to stand behind or beside. But being self-actualized is not to be perfect (in fact it is to abandon perfectionism), simply to know that one can be better.

A self-actualized person also has the clarity to see their own shortcomings and work to resolve them. They have the growth mindset which allows them to change and grow even after having achieved self-actualization. But remember that self-actualization is a growth need.

It all comes together so neatly, doesn't it?

That brings us from needs to desires. Here's where things get fun!

DESIRE

Derived from *desiderare*, Latin for *to wish or long for*, desire is our constant companion in ways great and small. It's a part of our life in every way, and it can be both inspirational or destructive.

Sigmund Freud (1856-1939) divided desires into roughly two categories of urges, libidinal (sexual) and aggressive (death). When each is suppressed, sexual urges often create productive or creative results while death urges often inspire depression or other destructive behaviors. He also noted that there could be some overlap, with sexual urges often becoming aggressive and death urges often having sexual undertones. Years later, the spectrum of strange and violent video images available on the internet bears this out.

Before we go any further, let's say simply what desires are not; needs. We've already looked at those, which are necessary for a fulfilled life. Desires are things beyond those needs which we crave, things we want.

When we lack desire, our lives are consumed only by necessity, and that is not a well-balanced life. Desire motivates us, and without it we can become bored or aimless and endlessly dissatisfied. This can lead to depression, poor health and sleeping habits, related physical and psychological complications leading to early death or even suicide.

One problem is that, for the first few formative years of our lives, our needs and desires are basically the same, the basic physiological and safety needs. A child both needs and desires food and drink and can't differentiate one inspiration from another. Then, when we mature, we often can't let go of that childhood parallel of need and desire. To the untrained, undisciplined mind, need and desire are still one. And so, one may feel they need a new car, or can't live without that pair of shoes. They've neglected the difference.

This is particularly striking in intimate relationships. You may come to need each other financially but not desire each other. You may feel you need an extra-monogamous partner, when this may simply be a desire. Do you need an apology, or do you simply desire one? It's a critical criteria for choosing what to ask for and how to ask for it.

You can always use an if/then construct to figure it out:

> *What if I don't get this, then what will happen?*
> *What if I do have this affair, then how will I feel?*
> *What if this doesn't happen, then what will I do?*

It helps you visualize the future and gives you clarity to make a better choice.

THE PROBLEMS OF DESIRE

Now that we're clear on our needs and, in this case, our desires, let's take a closer look at this complex and often contradictory impulse.

It's not surprising, perhaps, that the life force desire is known roughly as *destroyer of self-realization and knowledge* and *the great symbol of sin* in the Hindu tradition. Buddhism's Four Noble Truths proclaims lust, itself one of the purest forms of desire, is the cause of all suffering. The Old Testament's Adam and Eve had desire for knowledge, and we all remember how *that* worked out.

Still, let's take a more contemporary view.

We are taught early on that we must control our impulses. Sigmund Freud introduced the psychological model of the id, the ego, and the superego. In this model, the id is the part of the brain which is ruled by desire. This the impulsive, childhood part of the psyche which seeks immediate fulfilment without thought of others or of the future. The ego is the practical part of the psyche, the part which deals with the outside world and knows what is required, what is needed. The ego must govern the selfish, impulsive id. This is the central struggle of the psyche, the need of practicality wrestling with the wants of selfishness.

Only when the ego has gained control of the id, when the practical psyche has firm control over irrational desire, can the superego be achieved. The superego looks beyond the self of the id, beyond the social practicality of the self, and looks outward and up, toward the moral and spiritual good. Freud would argue that a psyche which fails to govern its own impulses and desires can never attain a clear moral perspective.

It's important to keep in mind that all three elements are necessary, they work together. The ego does not crush the id, as the id serves great purpose to the psyche. The id brings spontaneity and whimsy, creativity, a lot of the traits of the self-actualized person. But the id must be governed by the ego, which also has a vital purpose. All three work together.

So, we're not here to demonize desire, only to better understand it so that we can better control it. This will help you better understand your partner's desires and deal with them more effectively as well.

THE CYCLES OF DESIRE

Though it can be said, and often is, that suffering can be framed in terms of desire. There's a cycle to this, and if you recognize the cycle in yourself or others, you'll be better equipped to interrupt it. It starts with desire, which is unmet. Unmet desire is painful, pain causes fear and anxiety of more pain. Fear and anxiety may disrupt desire or radically misplace it, causing more desires to go unmet, which causes more pain and that triggers more anxiety and fear, creating misplaced desires which cannot be met, and so forth.

Here's an example: You desire the company of an attractive individual, but this person is married so your desires must go unmet. It's a reasonable position, but pain is an emotion and not a reason, so you feel the pain of the unmet desire. Now you may fear that no partner will accept you, you may have anxiety about what you might have done differently or what you still might do to change the outcome. This may give you the desire to interfere with the marriage, derail it in order to irradicate the problem. But that's not going to work, your desires will only go unmet. You're likely to have anxiety about what you've done, and fear of retribution. Looking for a clear conscience, you decide to move to another town. But your conscience will never be truly clean, so that desire goes unmet. It's an even worse pain to know what kind of decisions you've made, you're fearful that your life is ruined and anxious about what to do next. You desire a drink with the desire of somehow eliminating the pain. The next morning, that desire goes unmet, and so on.

It may sound extreme, but these things do happen. You might know somebody with a similar story. But that really doesn't matter to us. What about you? What are your desires? Might they lead you down this path? Try a few if/then exercises to know you're not heading down a dangerous and destructive path.

There's another destructive cycle of desire to be cautious of, one which is just as insidious. Desire can be a motivator; for success, for achievement of all sorts. We desire a big home, a nice car, a good job, an attractive partner.

But once these things are attained, all too often they become obsolete, insufficient. The same drive may push an individual to desire a bigger house, a nicer car, a better job, a more attractive partner.

The problem here is that one may fail to recall that desire is a motivator, it is not the goal. Desire feeding itself will never be satisfied. Once the objects of desire have been achieved, the energy of desire should be redirected; a desire to be charitable, a desire to help others, a desire to find greater forms of expression.

Because too often the things we desire are material things. This desire can blind us to what really motivated us in the first place, the things that truly matter. A person may desire the trappings of success, but to what end? Self-actualization, growth. But desire upon desire is not grown, it's just expansion. That's sideways growth, and it's really the same thing as going nowhere at all.

This kind of desire quickly becomes greed, and despite what Gordon Gecko and I said before, greed is *not* good.

THE WORLD AS WILL

Arthur Schopenhauer's *The World as Will* draws human society into two layered worlds; above is the world of appearances and, beneath that, lay the world of will. The world of appearances is the conscious world, the ego-driven world. The world of will is a blind process in the search for survival and reproduction. Schopenhauer tells us that the will is the formative world, the world of appearances merely a cluster of manifestations of that will.

Even the human body is designed to manifest the world of will. The mouth and stomach are hunger made manifest, genitals are the fundamental form of lust and desire to procreate. Nothing in the natural world can be separated by the will which inspires it.

This world of appearances is meant to appeal to our intellectual sides, we too are merely manifestations of our own will.

What does this mean to you? If world as will theory holds, everything in your world of appearances is really just a manifestation of your will. We've already discussed how the environment reflects and influences our mental state (see how it all comes together?) and now we see that concept taken to the limit. The environment isn't merely a reflection of the psyche, it is created by the will, subject entirely to its power. In this construct, it's a one-way exertion of influence.

Does your world reflect your will? What is that will? Put that will through the 5 Whys technique or a few if/then exercises to get to know that will better. But you may not have to do more than take a simple look around your immediate environment. Isn't your computer a manifestation of your will to succeed? What about those video files you downloaded? What part of your will do they manifest?

So, according to the World as Will concept, we don't shape our desires, our desires shape us. We can't choose them; we can only come to understand them and thereby control them. And as lofty as this theory is, it does make a lot of sense. Think about it; tastes and desires are formed when we're children and they rarely change; they're imprinted in our formative years. You like what you like, you want what you want, what turns you on simply is what turns you on. You can't really change it and you shouldn't deny it either, just understand it.

It's not always easy to understand our desires, as they are very often only in our subconscious minds. And we often are conflicted and even troubled when those desires become conscious. Conflicted sexuality or gender identification is a good example of this.

TYPES OF DESIRE

Desires rarely occur on their own. In fact, there are two types of desire and they usually work together. There are *terminal desires* and *instrumental desires*. Instrumental desires act in support of terminal desire. For instance, if I want to go get something to eat (a terminal desire) I desire to get dressed and find my car keys (instrumental desires).

Terminal desires are generated by feelings, in this case hunger. That makes them powerful desires. Instrumental desires are more reason-oriented and less impacting on our psyches. They're also more fleeting by nature, as it may take a dozen instrumental desires to get to one terminal desire. Instrumental desires are not intended for our pleasure, but the terminal desire is. Some desires are both instrumental and terminal, such as your career (if you enjoy it) or your home.

Both terminal and instrumental desires are considered healthy, positive desires.

Most terminal desires are also known as *hedonic* desires, which leads to pleasure in avoidance of pain. The craving for a cocktail is a hedonic desire, for example. Not all terminal pleasures are hedonic, however; there's the desire to be charitable, for example. Some may argue that any thing enjoyed is hedonic because you derive some pleasure from it, but I'm skeptical of such a jaded perspective.

Desires can also be divided into two other categories; *natural* and *unnatural*. The physiological desires are natural desires and are limited by their nature. Hunger is a desire sated by feeding, thirst by drinking. Unnatural desires, for power or fame or wealth, are unlimited. The desire for these things will never be sated. To paraphrase Epicurus, natural desires easy and pleasurable to be satisfied, so they should be satisfied. Unnatural desires are neither easy nor pleasurable to satisfy, so they shouldn't be.

A Fifteenth century Indian poet and philosopher Kabir described desire as constituting humanity's true wealth. Kabir believed that the person with the most desires were the poorest and seldom succeeded. Kabir considered them the saddest and most superficial of people, overwhelmed with too many desires which are of too little value.

Others are born with the same desires, but focus on only a few and manage to achieve at least some of them. These people are happier and considered successful.

A third group are born with fewer desires, and naturally focus on excelling at them and accomplish their goals to achieve their desires. These become great world leaders, scientists, and artists.

The rarest individual has only one desire, for transcendence. We've already seen how lofty a goal that is. And Kabir tells us that as emotional development grows, the number of desires decreases. Meditation (which we already touched on briefly) is a good way to reduce ten thoughts to five, five to two, two to one. This is one way meditation helps achieve transcendence. And anybody can meditate if they have just a few minutes, even one minute of focusing on your natural breath can be beneficial. You may not transcend, but it's a good start.

There's a direct correspondence between emotional development and desire quantity. Those with many desires are emotionally volatile. They're not committed to much, including their own emotions, so they don't last. However, just as feelings of anger pass quickly, so do feelings of joy or satisfaction.

People with fewer desires tend to have more passion. They have more energy to spread out over fewer pursuits and are more likely to succeed and achieve.

When all goals and desires meld, Kabir calls it *singular passion devotion*. This is the true goal of self-actualization, when all needs and desires are satisfied by the same pleasurable satisfaction.

Which type of person are you? If you feel you're overwhelmed by too many desires, make a few lists ranking them in importance, on a scale from one to ten. Leave yourself only the three which you are most likely to accomplish. They don't have to be the three most vital or most challenging. Achieve those desires and move on to another three. You may also consider cutting a few, either those that are too grand or too petty.

What stage of desire do you find yourself in? Are your emotions volatile? That could be a sign that your desires are too many and you have to pair them down. Get out your pen and start making some lists!

Though meditation is a good way to do that, suffering is another. Those who suffer more desire less and focus on what's truly important in life, forgoing unnatural desires. First-responders, combat veterans and other POWs are good and honorable examples.

3

WHY: DEALING WITH ROOT CAUSES

While it's vital to know how to conduct yourself when communicating in your intimate relationships (and any relationships really), it's time to go deeper. We must look past *how* we are communicating and even past *what* we are saying, and go all the way to the root causes, the *why* of what we're saying, feeling, and doing.

Any personal transformation starts with the center of the body and soul. The existential questions of a person's self-dentification, of their place in society, are central to who they are and what they think on virtually every level. (We'll get back to existentialism later in this chapter.) A person with a fixed mindset who self-identifies as a loser, they will only embark on a downward spiral into self-fulfilling prophecy, missing out on opportunities, overthinking things and demanding perfection which is unattainable. A person with a growth mindset who sees themselves as resilient will likely be resilient, and they'll overcome failure to achieve great success.

So, this is one of our core concepts, the things from which other attitudes and behavior springs.

But it's not the only one.

SIGNS AND ROOT CAUSES OF NEUROTIC BEHAVIOR

The term *neurotic behavior* is as broad as it is misunderstood. It may sound like a cheap insult, a catch-all diagnosis for someone's behavior you may not like, or for a person you may not like. But it includes a number of very serious conditions. So, if we're going to get to the root of miscommunication and the other things which destroy relationships and even entire lives, a little time must be spent on neurotic behavior.

You might be inclined to skip this section, but I strongly recommend you don't. A lot of people exhibit neurotic behavior, and in ways they may not even understand. And even if you don't consider yourself neurotic, your partner may exhibit these behaviors, and the whole purpose of this book is to arm you with the tools you'll need to deal with a variety of challenges, neuroses included.

Neuroses are not psychoses. To be admittedly quite general about it, a psychotic loses the ability to distinguish fantasy from reality. The neurotic is actually hypersensitive to reality. A true psychotic may believe they are being followed or conspired against, though there is no conspiracy. A neurotic is more concerned with germs; and while there are germs, their danger is imagined.

The tricky part is that there is a lot of crossover. Disorders like borderline personality and bipolar may seem more like neuroses, but they go much deeper. Some believe borderline personality disorder can't be treated at all.

But there are some common signs to keep an eye on if you're looking out for neurotic behavior.

One common neurotic behavior is unstable emotions. Neurotics can fly into a rage (also common to bipolar disorder.) Another common neurotic behavior is a so-called addictive personality. The research is all over the map as to the roots of an addictive personality, and it could have as much to do with parental imprinting as it does with a chemical imbalance in the brain. Both could be true. But surely, addictions are a neurotic behavior. The neurotic is hyper sensitive to the pressure of life; overwork, boredom, negative self-talk or a negative self-image, a sense of futility which comes with a closed mindset. But it's a big red flag for neurotic behavior either way.

Perfectionism is a classic neurosis. Hyper-sensitive to reality, a perfection for a sese of control, to define his- or herself in the best possible terms. Anything short of that may nag at them, rob them of the joy of their efforts and prevent new efforts. Perfectionists, like others on this list, tend to go toward negative self-talk and overthinking, the replaying of previous events or the imagining of upcoming or possible events. This plagues perfectionists, fixed-minded folks of all sorts, and it's a very common neurotic behavior. If you overthink things, you can easily deal with this by accepting your imperfection and the chaotic nature of the world, let go of the past and the future and live only in the present. Meditate. But beware of this deadly duo of perfectionism and overthinking.

Chronic stress is also a common neurotic behavior. We all get stressed out now and then, but if a person is constantly stressed then they probably lack the coping skills, and they should read this book. Chronic stress is a common result of overthinking. And like a lot of these neurotic behaviors, stress can have terrible effects on the body. Internal inflammation, a common result of stress, can cause heart attacks and strokes. Behaviors associated with common stress are also common to the others; food and substance abuse and the health risks that go along with it, including premature death. Stress and other of these neuroses have psychological effects too, including depression, sleep disruption, and suicide.

Envy is a neurotic behavior. It creates obsessions of inferiority and jealousy and pent-up resentment and may inspire kleptomania and other anti-social behavior. Those who exhibit envy are often fixed-minded people, more concerned with how they appear to others, successful or not, more than how they see the world.

Being over-dramatic, which we've already touched on, is a classic neurotic behavior. It happens as a result of excessive sadness or anger, often rooted in some small problem. But it results in a fit of rage, a temper tantrum which the person often can't control. At least they never learned to; they could if they tried. But this kind of overacting is a leading cause of breakups, and it's also a very common neurotic behavior. It's also wildly anti-social. Forget losing your love relationship, if you're a temperamental person to outbursts of rage, it won't be long until you're entirely alone.

Hopelessness is a common neurotic behavior too, in a lot of ways it's the flipside of being over dramatic. It leads to depression, substance abuse, and suicide. But starts off simply enough, just an extended melancholy born of a fixed mindset which is certain that nothing will ever work out. Well, if you were dead sure nothing would ever work out, you'd probably be feeling hopeless too. But hopelessness can be related to stress, to a passing crisis like an illness or the death of a friend or loved one. I can be born of disappointment, the loss of a job or a romance. But it can also self-sabotage a career or a relationship. Nobody wants to be around a sad sack Debbie Downer, right?

NEUROTIC BEHAVIOR'S OWN ROOTS

But neurotic behavior is more than just deep-rooted and liable to cause all manner of other problems, it can also be traced back to other behaviors and conditions. Some people believed, and many still do, that neuroses are genetic, handed down from one generation to the next, symptomatic of disorders like schizophrenia. Many more modern researchers believe they're acquired behaviors. Traumas are often cited as the root of various neuroses, and others are the result of parental imprinting.

Child abuse is a common cause of many neuroses, including perfectionism and chronic stress. A lot of adults live striving to correct whatever mistakes they made in the past to inspire the abuses of their childhood.

Because neurotic behavior is so widespread and varied and often hard to identify, it's a much more widespread problem than it need be. And with our recently turbulent world, there's even more anxiety and the neurotic behaviors which are likely to result.

As long as we're looking at the part neuroses play in our lives and in how and what we communicate, especially to our romantic partners, we should go one step further. Because once you've looked at some of the neurotic behaviors, let's take a look at some of the even more deeply rooted complexes which are often associated. Not by coincidence, these are also among the most commonly reported complexes blamed for failed relationships in various studies.

The Oedipus/Electra Complex is when a person has an almost sexual attraction to the parent of the opposite gender.

A deep affection for the parent of the opposite sex. Oedipus, of Ancient Greek myth, fell in love with his mother and killed his father. Electra, on the other hand, was attracted to her father and blamed her mother. These days, the complexes are a lot more conservative in nature. But there are many cases where an unnaturally strong bond between mother and son (for example) can result in an emotionally stunted adult child unable to truly step into an adult role. It's also a common killer of romantic relationships. No woman wants to deal with that, and why would she? This complex leads to perfectionism and overthinking as the child fixates on the parent with eternal efforts to impress and win their love and approval. It can lead to a lot of negative self-talk and overthinking as the frustrated child constantly scolds his- or herself over failures to do better, to truly win that parent's love.

It's a shame, because a more growth-oriented mindset would help the adult child abandon the fixed mindset they may have acquired during childhood; that the child is and should always be the central figure in the parent's life. As a result, these adult children tend to treat their adult partners poorly; neither can live up to their unreasonable childhood expectations, which themselves are doomed for disappointment. Men may abuse their partners; women may retire from social interaction entirely.

The Madonna/whore complex is a way to describe the perspective of men who see women as being one of two archetypes; a virginal young mother (the Madonna) and a ravenous, sexual beast (the whore). The complex has been played out in countless works of fiction and comedy; it's driven into our collective conscience. You need go no further than Ginger and Mary Ann of the 1960s sitcom *Gilligan's Island*. They were the Madonna/whore complex come to life, and it was and remains powerful iconography.

Another, more modern take on the complex states that men with this complex truly desire both archetypes in one person, a schoolteacher by day and a stripper by night. They're meant to be all things and also in turn.

Men who suffer from this complex are often unable to maintain a relationship because few women are either one of the extreme types, and fewer more are actually a combination of both, which is what a lot of men truly want. This unrealistic expectation is, as most, almost always doomed to end in disappointment.

Men also seem to have a hard time differentiating one aspect from the other, and the whore persona may contaminate the school-teacher/homemaker side of her dual persona. Or he may want only the whore but discover she is much more that that. He may feel cheated, but of course he was only let down by his unrealistic expectation.

Men with this complex are often alone and lonely, imbued with desire and vision but with no reasonable way to find satisfaction. This man is often of a fixed mindset, seeing women as one type or the other, his own situation eternally stifled. Perfectionism is also a red flag for this common complex.

The God complex can be particularly irksome for lovers. One of the two may consider themselves answerable to nobody. It's their way or the highway. Not only are these people commonly arrogant to the point of being insufferable, they're prone to perfectionism, other complexes like the aforementioned Madonna/whore complex, believing they deserve it all, and all of it perfect. But this person may also be prone to infidelity. So, if your partner leans toward a God complex, be on your guard. Really, any of these common complexes should probably put you on your guard.

Someone with a persecution complex has an irrational fear of hated, mistreated, persecuted. This complex, related to paranoia, is common among overthinkers and those with negative self-images. It leads to chronic stress, self-medication, an exaggerated panic reflex, and sleep deprivation. And in relationships, a person with this condition will be suspicious of the other, they'll project their insecurities onto the behavior of the other. Very often, this person will suspect the other of something themselves have done or might do; the liar imagines everyone else lying, the thief will suspect you of stealing, the cheater will assume you're doing the same thing. It's almost always unreasonable and irrational and can kill a relationship as fast and as certain as anything else.

Those with a martyr complex rely on suffering for sympathy and attention. The martyr appears selfless, but the longsuffering soon become the longwinded. Those who go on about their sacrifices are really just languishing in self-pity. Often, they're making excuses or blaming others for a lack of their own achievements. The martyr will never take responsibility for themselves. The sufferer of this complex is often of a fixed mindset, believing they must always play that role, that it is the only way they can get ahead. But they're often afraid of trying, afraid of failure, and wracked with a lack of self-confidence and little confidence in the notions of change or progress.

This person can be insufferable to an intimate partner, robbing their relationship of its joy to replace it with the guilt and drama that they martyr complex requires.

The inferiority complex leaves a person feeling unable to succeed or even survive. They feel they just don't have it in them and they never will, that they're destined for failure. And the law of the self-fulfilling prophecy suggests that, sadly, they're right. This is a kind of perfectionism turned on its ear, call it *imperfectionism* if you will. The sufferer is so vastly convinced of failure, perfectionism is so far from them, they can only see their own imperfections, the imperfections in their lives and their futures.

People who suffer this complex often suffer depression, lifestyle issues, physical and psychological issues stretching across the spectrum.

The flipside to the inferiority complex is the superiority complex. This person believes they're naturally superior, not inferior. Also, a perfectionist, this person may see everything they do as perfect. Similar to the God complex.

Those with a guilt complex blame themselves for everything and anything which may go wrong. Just as the inferiority and superiority complexes are closely associated, and the superiority complex is a close cousin to the God complex, the guilt complex can be hard to differentiate from the inferiority complex.

The man with the Don Juan complex sees women strictly as a source of pleasure. This is a womanizer with no interest in long-term relationships. I'm sure there are instances of this with women who suffer the same complex with men. The condition is actually called hypersexual disorder, sometimes called sex addiction. These people are often emotionally distant, overthinkers, and they're just not good candidates for a monogamous relationship.

Lastly, there is the hero complex, wherein the person, man or woman, positions themselves at the center of attention by virtue of their accomplishments. Often indulging in false humility, the person with the hero complex brags about his or her accomplishments (this is what the term *humblebrag* means). This person is often fixed-minded, as they put the focus on the individual's qualities instead of the final result and the common good. The hero complex is not apt to be generous with sharing credit, and can seem selfish and self-promoting, because they are. The person with a hero complex is not likely to be a good listener, or to be empathetic, since so much of their attention is on themselves. The hero complex is similar to the superiority and the God complexes, and in a way to the martyr complex, which also seeks to draw the full attention of the others. In fact, a closer look reveals that all of these complexes put the person at the center of the action, from various angles and in both various and consistent ways.

Whatever the complex or cause, there is a handy, almost-universally known way to get to the bottom of it, and that's something you should know before we move even further into the root causes of ineffective communication in relationships.

THE 5 WHYS

Back in the 1930s so-called *father of the Japanese industrial revolution*, and Toyota Industries, needed a way to make work at his factories more efficient. He developed the now-famous *5 Whys* system. If any worker were to come across a challenge, they only needed to ask why to five consecutive answers. His theory is that one is never more than five steps from finding the root cause to any problem. It was then a matter of resolving the fifth answer.

Here's an example to make things a little easier:

A worker has arrived late to work. The first question is, "Why?" That's *why* number one.

A (1): "I couldn't get onto the factory grounds."

Q (2): "Why?"
A (2): "The man wouldn't open the gate."

Q (3): "Why?"
A (3): "It was malfunctioning."

Q (4): "Why?"
A (4): "It wasn't serviced properly or promptly."

Q (5): "Why?"
A (5): "Because the country has not set aside a budget for maintenance."

The root of the problem, setting aside budget money for maintenance of the gates, can now be solved.

Let's try it when it comes to something more contemporary and perhaps more relevant to you. One person may ask another, "You're upset, honey? Why?"

A (1): "I'm depressed."

Q (2): "Why?"
A (2): "I lost my job."

Q (3): "Why?"
A (3): "My poor performance."

Q (4): "Why?"
A (4): "I've been partying a lot lately."

Q (5): "Why?"
A (5): "I just can't stop drinking."

It's an amazingly effective technique, one you can use at any time, on the spot and one with which you can find the resolution to virtually any puzzle or quandary. It should help you in helping your friends or partners in crisis as well.

EXISTENTIAL ANSWERS?

Remember when I said we'd come back to existentialism? Well, here we are. Any philosophy poses a question: What is the nature of the heavens? What is the nature of mankind? When these questions are answered, they cease to become philosophies and become sciences (in this case astronomy and biology).

But the prominent philosophy of the Twentieth century, existentialism, will never become science because its questions are so particular to the individual: Who am I? What is my purpose in life? When those questions are answered, lives may be secured, but not sciences. The reason is obvious; unlike the mechanics of the Universe or of the human body, the answers to the existential questions are different for every person who asks.

Existentialism was born in the Age of Enlightenment at the end of the Nineteenth century (romantic-era writer Mary Shelley's *Franken-*

stein is an early existentialist tome). But existentialism came of age in the mid-Twentieth century as a result of the horror of World War II. The cruelties of the German concentration camps led many to believe that there could be no God if such horrors could go on.

Later existentialist philosophers like Kierkegaard, Nietzsche, and Sartre, believed that life had no purpose, and so nobody had any real purpose either. We're born, we live, we have suffering and pleasure, perhaps we marry and procreate, and we die. No heaven, no purpose, just mold clinging to a rock floating around in the cold vacuum of space.

Fun crowd.

But few of us can afford to be so detached. We have to live our busy lives and find some reason to keep on keepin' on. To think we're working so hard for pretty much nothing is more than a lot of people can stand. Anxiety is a common symptom, as is depression, negative self-talk, overthinking, and a lot of other negative behaviors.

Existential psychology examines these connections between mental health and existential crisis. Research into patients with a range of issues and personality disorders as well as terminal illnesses such as cancer revealed a strange common denominator. They longed to maintain meaningful and truly nurturing relationships with others. Instead, they tended to use their relationships to cope with existential anxieties.

Existential anxieties tend to take root during youth and may last a lifetime. Isolation constantly recalls the suffer that they were born and will die alone. A fixed mindset and negative self-talk assures the sufferer that living alone is natural and inevitable. Freedom reminds us that we are unrooted, disconnected. Feelings of meaninglessness are only strengthened by years of searching for a purpose which we may never find simply by virtue of our certainty that meaning and purpose are illusory.

Luckily, we have a handy remedy! Use the 5 Whys technique to move away from the puzzle of the crisis and get to the root of it. Take more than the five if you need to, but if you keep asking why, which is a fundamental question in existentialism, the simple answer will slowly come to you.

The patient can't sleep and has constant anxiety, and the doctor asks the first *why:*

> A (1): "I'm afraid I'm going to die alone."
>
> Q (2): "Why?"
> A (2): "Because I can't find a spouse."
>
> Q (3): "Why?"
> A (3): "Because I'm unlovable."
>
> Q (4): "Why?"
> A (4): "Because I'm so messed up."
>
> Q (5): "Why?"
> A (5): "Because life has no meaning."

And there's the solution! If your life has no meaning, find some meaning for it. Volunteer a food bank and you'll realize that to help others is one of the things that gives life meaning. It's hard work and that'll help you sleep, which will make you more pleasant and alert. And that will come in happy when you meet a likeminded single at the food bank, who perhaps was also just looking for a little meaning in their lives.

I mentioned *Frankenstein* earlier, and it raises an interesting point. The creature asks the existential question of his own identity, but he allows society to define him as a monster and so he becomes a monster. He does not answer the existential questions for himself. But existentialism fairly well demands the seeker find a solution before society does, or the self-actualized mind can never be achieved.

And this brings us to our next chapter, WHO. You may think you know the answers to that, and what you've learned in this book so far may have enlightened you even further and sent you on a voyage of self-discovery that will change your life. Bravo or brava, my friend! But knowing about narrative therapy will make your journey a lot easier and less perilous. It's a significant advance for almost anyone in mental or emotional crisis, but it's ideally suited for applications in the area of relationships.

4

WHO: NARRATIVE THERAPY IN COUPLES' COMMUNICATION

You may never have heard of narrative (or cognitive) therapy, as it is a modern school of mental health treatment. I use *narrative* because the focus is on the narrative of the person's life. A person's expressions of the stories of their life experiences shape their view of themselves in the context of those experiences, of that story, of that narrative.

The key to narrative therapy is that people tend to tell themselves this story of their lives time and time again, reaffirming that narrative and their place within it. It's a fixed mindset which is secure that no change is possible.

They may see themselves as a loser, for example, after years of losing significant things in their lives; parents, lovers, jobs, opportunities. In answering the existential question of identity and purpose, this person has answered the question and resolved themselves to the answer. In their version of *Frankenstein*, they are the creature, the wretch.

Others may see themselves as the doctor, young Victor. Victor's best intentions create a set of circumstances he cannot control. How many of us have that feeling of helplessness, hopelessness, that we'll fail no matter what we do? It's reminiscent of the martyr complex and both the inferiority and the superiority complexes and, in its own way, the God complex too.

Some may see themselves as the Victor's betrothed, Elizabeth, a victim of male abuse which has made her ugly, wretched, worthy of death.

Not that everybody sees themselves through the prism of this particular story. Everybody has their own story of which they are the central character. Charles Dickens' great *David Copperfield* begins: *Whether I shall turn out to be the hero of my own life, or whether that station will be held by anybody else, these pages must show.* Sometimes we are the villains of our lives, sometimes the fool.

But this role is not prescribed, even by the pattern of one's experiences. A fixed-minded person would tend to see the pattern as determinative of the future, a fatalistic view which abandons responsibility. A growth-minded person sees the narrative as fluid, the role subject to interpretation, that failure can lead to success.

In a nutshell, not only can a person change their role in the middle of their life's story, from fool to hero, but they can rewrite the entire narrative to change the character from the very start. Changing the narrative changes the role and that changes the perspective and that changes the life.

Developed by Michael White and David Epston in the 1980s, narrative therapy separates a person from their behavior. This way a person who committed a crime can identify themselves as a person who made a mistake, not a criminal and therefore, unworthy of a normal and happy life.

This therapeutic model features three main conceptual protocols. It is respectful, treating clients as individuals and not the sum of their mistakes. The approach is likewise non-blaming, focusing on outside factors and the influence of circumstance and deflecting any sense of blame or shame against the client. Lastly, narrative therapy views the client as the expert. In narrative therapy, the subject comes to the conclusions through a series of answers. The client is never instructed or dissected; they are guided to discover these things for themselves.

Now wouldn't your next emotional or intimate conflict benefit from just that paragraph alone? Worth the price of admission right there. But there's more!

Narrative therapy distinguishes between an individual who has problems with an individual who is problematic. It's an important difference, because an individual with problems can correct those problems, they can be changed. The problematic individual cannot be changed.

Here's how narrative therapy keeps the focus on the difference between the problem and the person.

Our interactions with others impact the way we experience reality. That reality is communicated through and influenced by language. Different languages can actually influence different interpretations of the same events or experiences. Stories and narrative help us understand reality and our place in it, answering the basic existential questions.

Narrative therapy focuses on subjective realities. Instead of an objective reality or truth, the truth is interpretive. And it is accepted that one person may interpret an event one way and someone else another.

It's akin to postmodernism, a school of thought which holds that there's no objective truth, that reality is changing, shifting, a personal concept instead of a shared set of facts. Norms and facts have their place, but they're more influential than causal.

So narrative therapy sees individuals in a postmodern context. There is no universal reality, the truth belongs to the individual, who creates his own reality. And, lest anyone suffer the sad fate of Frankenstein's creature, he or she must construct that reality, or allow the pains of letting somebody else construct it instead, to suffer the consequences.

Narrative therapy provides these very same story-retelling skills.

COMMON NARRATIVE THERAPY TECHNIQUES

The first step is telling the story by putting together a narrative. The therapy seeks to help the client find their voice to tell their own story (or this might be you). Storytelling is the way a person may find meaning and purpose from our own personal experiences.

The story may need guidance through questions to discover for themselves the meaning and the healing and to recreate a new identity, and reshape the narrative. A narrative can be altered, flipped on its head, or rewritten altogether. Interpretation can create countless narratives from a single narrative, as we saw with *Frankenstein*.

The second step is the *externalization technique*, which separates the questionable problems or even behaviors around the client from the client. The problem is not the person. And it's easier to change what you do than who you are. So, separate the two and fix the easiest one first. It's easier to change your behavior than your feelings, we've already seen that; same thing here only more so.

If you're quick to anger, for example, that's behavior. If you see yourself as an angry person, that's something else again. Learn not to be so temperamental, change your behavior, and you'll change your identity as a temperamental person. Change the behavior, change your persona.

It all sounds very theoretical, but it really works. Let's look at a few other techniques of applying narrative therapy, and then we'll get down to the emotional communication aspect of it all.

The third technique is the *deconstruction technique*, which deconstructs a problem to reduce it to insignificant parts. It's another way to break down a big task into smaller tasks, classic technique for a variety of applications. It also gives almost anyone the chance to see the bigger picture, the forest for the trees.

Deconstructing can reduce overgeneralizing and make an issue more-specific and easy to handle while clarifying core issues. It can really bring you to the core of almost any issues, and it works well integrated with the *5 Whys* technique, which can be helpful here, as it is on so many occasions.

The *unique outcomes technique* is the way one changes their own storyline. It's a way to reframe their experiences, which you cannot change, into a different interpretation, which you can change. You can turn a living nightmare into a life-affirming story of survival, a victim into a hero, just by adjusting the perspective even slightly. And it's more than just positive thinking, it's changing the entire worldview. It's not avoiding the problem, its reimagining it.

And this technique can include multiple storylines as well, for us and for others involved in our stories. Remember, there is no objective truth in this school of thought, and that leaves a lot of room for subjective truth. And a disaster in one narrative may seem insignificant in another narrative, so the possibilities of this approach are expansive, if not endless.

I'll bet you figured that existentialism would be the last big technique of narrative therapy. It re-asks the questions of identity and purpose, allowing the client (or your friend or yourself) to change their minds about who they are and answer it in a different way, a way which will shape their lives in a positive and not a negative way.

Here's a great narrative therapy exercise you or anyone else can do. It may be extremely helpful, and it just might be a little bit fun.

Imagine you're writing your life's story. This will help you separate yourself from the events of your past and giving you a wider perspective of those experiences and your life as a whole. Now do the table of contents; seven chapters which encapsulate major eras in your life. Then come up with at least one subhead, or a line which describes what the chapter is about. You can use this book as an example!

But you might write something like:

I GUESS I DESERVED IT I GOT A TERRIBLE DISEASE AND DIED ALONE

Expressive Arts are the third principal technique of narrative therapy. We all have different ways of expressing ourselves. Some are visual, some audio-oriented. Painting and sculpture work just the same way, or even interpretive dance. This technique works great with kids, but it could work great with intimate companions as well, as it provides fun and interactive practices. Art is well-known to have positive energy and various therapeutic powers.

Yoga and meditation are great shared and private activities which can help anyone redefine themselves and change their narrative.

Visualization is a powerful technique. Imagine the new narrative, the new character, the new future. Write it in your mind or on a vision board. That's another fun shared activity to draw or keep a couple together. Make sure to include your partner on your vision board!

So, how do you put narrative therapy to use? Try encouraging answers with some questions like these: "It sounds like this problem might be a part of your life. How long have you noticed this? What effect does it have on you and your life? Does this affect your energy or distract you from your daily duties? Does this impact your daily life? Does it affect your child's life, or your partner's?"

Remember to differentiate the problem from the person with questions like, "Do you accept the effect of this problem? If you do, why? If not, why not? Why do you take that position?"

Remember to keep things moving forward, toward a new narrative and a new future with questions like, "What would you prefer? How would you rearrange things if you could? What do you think you might do to rearrange these things so that they'd be as you prefer?"

So, when you're speaking to your intimate partner, your romantic intended, or just about anybody, you can always start such a conversation in this way (or something like it):

"Do you remember the last time this wasn't a problem? What did that feel like? What happened at that time, in those first few minutes, and what happened after that?"

Then move on from the past to the future, make it constructive. *"Do you want more moments like that? What can we do in order to recreate those things now? How would you feel if we did those things?"*

It comes to another type of visualization of the future, a technique we've already seen to be powerful and motivational.

But how can you use all this in your own intimate relationships? It's really simpler than it seems. Is your partner serially unfaithful? Instead of being accusatory or confrontive, you adopt the narrative therapy techniques of being non-blameful and separating the person from the deed. This is not a serial cheater, but a person who makes the same bad choice over and over again. What are the reasons for this behavior? Perhaps there are triggers which can be avoided by a slight alteration of behavior. What feelings do these behaviors inspire in your partner? Can they envision a different set of circumstances which might create a different inspiration and so, change their own behavior? Can you imagine something else which might give you the same feeling? How do you or your partner see yourselves in that circumstance, when they're being unfaithful? How do they see themselves? Is that how they want to feel? Do they want to change the circumstance so that they can feel differently?

The client is expert and with the right guidance they can find the answers.

But it's as important to ask yourself these questions as it is to ask anyone else. You may be trapped in a narrative that constrains you. Remember that narrative therapy is not about blame, but about accepting reasonable responsibility and being willing to act on it and pro-actively make the necessary changes.

NARRATIVE THERAPY AND COUPLES

We've already seen how narrative therapy allows us to reconsider our life stories and our places with that context. It allows us to externalize the person from the problem, and that helps clear up a lot of issues for individuals and couples alike.

Couples tend to see their problems as being part of their identities as a couple. The problems become internalized into their *couple-hood*, if you will. A person may believe that the problems in their lives come from within and are endemic *("I'm a criminal")* instead of external *("I'm a person who has made mistakes"),* a couple may come to feel the same about their pairing *("We're just a bad couple"* instead of *"we're good people with some relationship issues").*

In a couple's situation, many of the same techniques apply. The problems should be externalized, made separate from the identity of the clients. Even behaviors should be externalized, because behaviors can be changed.

Some behaviors do come up as a result of clashes of personalities. They both may be manager types and are overmanaging each other. One may have a complex which clashes with the other. In any case, those clashes can be externalized.

One trick anybody can use is to identify these problems and then call them by a name. It can be anything from The Beast to Prince Albert, it really doesn't matter. The point is that it makes the problem separate from the clients.

Questions are vital for a couple. Once separate from the problems, they must stick together as a couple to solve those problems. They may ask, "How can we change our behavior to resolve this issue? What kind of need or desire are we looking at?"

Blame, criticism, defensiveness, and closedmindedness are often problems between couples, but externalizing and questioning can help. You might try something like, "Is your anxiety rooted in trust issues about us? How does the criticism damage our relationship? Is blame threatening our shared dreams? Should we listen more to one another?"

Now that we've gone deep into the *What* of couples' communication, it's time to move on to the Where and the When, both of which are crucial to consider in greater depth.

5

WHEN: RECOGNIZING THE CRISIS POINT AND THE BREAKING POINT

Every relationship has little bumps along the way, every *life* does. So, putting two people together to share a life is, in reality, a matter of putting twice as many bumps on a single, shared road.

And in each case, the person or a couple may simply brush these things off. They may say, "Sure, I drink a little," or "We bump heads sometimes." And those things are acceptable in moderation. But when do these behaviors become a problem which has to be dealt with?

Of course, the best thing is to start off with an open line of communication from the very start. It's best not to let silent resentments build up, not ever to use blameful language or to be overtly confrontive. And we all go into our relationships believing this will be the case.

But if it were, you wouldn't be reading this right now.

It's possible that you're about to start off a new romance and you want to get off on a good foot. Excellent! Everything in this book will help you out. Maybe you're between relationships and you're determined not to fall into the same cycles the next time. Also, excellent! Be growth-minded and use this information to move onward toward your future successes.

It's also fairly likely that you are in a relationship right now and that you're urgently hoping to rescue it. Excellent. This book may help you do just that.

But how do you know if you're at that crisis point? Nobody wants to be the overthinking worrier so afraid of having a bad relationship that they enact a self-fulfilling prophecy and wind up creating a bad relationship from a good one. On the other hand, if you stand by and watch your relationship go sour, it's as much your fault as your partners because you failed to act when you could.

And just when *is* that?

THE CRISIS POINT

A breach of trust is not something you can ignore. It can be major, like cheating, or something like divulging a secret or humiliating your partner in public. It could be a money matter. One partner entrusts another with the safekeeping of these things, and violating that trust has to be dealt with.

On the one hand, it's very egregious behavior and it will not only continue but it will get worse if allowed to go unchecked. More money will disappear, more public humiliations will alienate partners and also friends.

On another hand, such things cause deep-rooted resentment which is sure to be corrosive to the relationship. That's not a bump in the road, it's a sinkhole.

Frequent arguing is a bad sign. Of course, couples disagree about things, and may even flare up from time to time. But if it's become a regular thing, it has to be dealt with. If you follow the guidance in this book, of course, you'll never have to have another argument again. But constant clashing has to be addressed. It's not healthy and it's not clear communication.

In fact, not having clear communication itself is a bad sign. Overt conflict isn't always the problem. Sometimes people just sort of shut down, then close up. When asked, everything's fine. But it's not, and it's only going to get worse. Complicating this is that some people close off, consciously or unconsciously, because they are self-sabotaging and creating a self-fulfilling prophecy. They won't communicate, and then they complain that there's no communication.

You might be doing that yourself, or your partner may be. Consider what one of you might be doing to encourage the other down this destructive path and how you can change your behavior in order to change course.

It might be a matter of something being wrong, but you just can't put your finger on what it is. That happens a lot. People are complicated and often emotional to the exclusion of being rational. They're generally resistant to change or compromise, they harbor all manner of complexes and exhibit a spectrum of negative behaviors.

Along the lines of a lack of communication, there may be something you want your partner to know, but you just can't bring yourself to say it. Maybe you're worried about their reaction, maybe you're not sure if you're right to bring it up.

Hey, it happens.

Have you figured out if it's a need or desire? What kind of need, what type of desire? Is it a natural desire or an unnatural desire? Those and other analytical techniques in this book should help you figure it out. But if you're wrestling with it, then there is definitely a communication problem somewhere along the line. Finding out where that blockage is will be your true challenge.

If either or even both of you become dysfunctional when you have a conflict, it's a big problem. Conflicts do arise, of course. But if one or the other or both start shouting, drinking, throwing things, slamming doors, and closing themselves off, that dysfunction needs to be addressed. It's probably a deeper-rooted issue than whatever the current argument is about.

Life-changing crises may create a breach between partners which needs to be addressed. The deaths of family members, loss of job or career, disease, these can throw a person into a different mindset. A formerly growth-minded person may become fixed minded in the face of grief for a devastating loss. They can readopt a growth mindset or retain the fixed mindset, that will be up to them. But great loss can create stunning changes in perspective and behavior.

Have you or your partner suffered a devasting loss? Keep that in mind when evaluating their behavior or your own. Make allowances, but don't let those changes become permanent. People often fall into these patterns if not corrected, while others fear rebuke if they are indelicate during moments of great loss. It's a high wire to walk, but it's also a long fall off of either side.

If you feel like you're stuck in patterns of harmful or negative behavior, it may be time to talk things out. Locked in a party cycle that's wearing you out? Do you find yourself engaging in negative self-talk more than you used to? These patterns have all kinds of ramifications and consequences and can send you both down a bad spiral, as individuals and as a couple. That's something you should talk out.

If there's a severe dip in your emotional intimacy, that's a problem that has to be addressed. Sure, no couple stays in the honeymoon period forever, that's fair enough. But there can also be a sudden chasm which may open up between two people well into their relationship. It could be because of something physical, like weight gain. But it may not be that one couple is repulsed by the other's weight gain, but that the person gaining weight is suddenly self-conscious and apprehensive. Or it could be due to an attraction to a third person, or any number of things. But emotional intimacy is crucial to a healthy romantic relationship, and one is not likely to survive without it. Don't let that go too far without addressing it.

Along the same lines (and probably in direct connection) is a dip in physical intimacy. These things work together, and the loss of one is almost certain to lead to a loss of the other, and if you lose both your relationship is in mortal danger. Physical intimacy, as we have seen, is what makes an intimate relationship so special. That's the thing you reserve only for your partner. You may share your charm or your experience or your grace, but not your physical intimacy. It has special value. That's why infidelity is so painful, because it destroys that thing about the other which is most rare and exclusive. The amount of trust, the importance of which we've already discussed, is greater when the risk is greater, and physical intimacy involves one of the greatest risks an individual can take in society.

When physical intimacy wanes, it creates insecurities, feelings of rejection which make them protective of their vulnerability to shut down further, close themselves off even more. That downward spiral is the death knoll of any intimate relationship.

RECOGNIZING THE BREAKING POINTS

We're here to help you either rescue, manage, or create an intimate relationship. And we're going to keep trying. The second section of this book is jam-packed with exercises, lists of things to do in order to bond or re-bond with your partner or future partners. You might have fun doing them alone!

Those are ways to identify and deal with the crisis points.

But for a moment, we have to take a look at what happens when a relationship just won't work out. Just as you have to know when to take a stand, when it's important to put effort into saving a relationship, you should also know when to walk away and invest your energies and passions elsewhere.

So, let's move from the crisis points to the breaking points.

THE BREAKING POINT

First of all, if you've been trying and trying, using all the techniques in this book, perhaps even gone to therapy, and there's no real progress, perhaps it's time to move on. You can't fit a square peg into a round hole no matter how hard you try.

We talked about abusive partners, who create abusive relationships. There are various types of abuse, including physical, sexual, psychological, and verbal. The basic cycle of abuse includes friendliness, anger, abuse, contrition. Things start off well enough (friendly), then somebody gets resentful and perhaps drunk (angry) then they let loose (abuse) and later they beg forgiveness (contrite). Once forgiven, they're friendly for a while, later angry, then abusive, and of course being contrite gives them license to repeat the cycle.

If you're the perpetrator of this cycle, you are an abuser. Your partner cannot help you, and the best I can do is to make you aware of what you're doing. Get serious help from a therapist. If you're the victim of this cycle, just get out. True, this abuser you're with may ultimately find good care and become a better person, but it's more than likely that they won't. And you should neither spend your life suffering under the abuse nor should you legitimize the abuse by playing the role of victim. Also, your leaving may be the only thing which jars the abuser enough to convince him or her to get the help they need. For your sake and your partner's, get out of an abusive relationship as soon and as quickly as you can.

If you know in your heart that there's just no future in the relationship, then what are you fighting for? If you know you don't want to marry the person, won't ever have children with them, if you know they love you and you're simply ambivalent, then you're not doing either one of you any favors. You're only making each other miserable and restricting yourself from finding better relationships with more fitting partners. Also, the longer you stay with somebody you know you'll be leaving, the more you're actually taking advantage of them, exploiting them for whatever they have to offer while you're waiting for the right next person to come along. Looking back, your partner is bound to feel lied to and abused. As they say, *when you know, you got to go.*

Different values and beliefs may also be insurmountable. You might have thought those religious differences wouldn't be a problem, but they may be coming up again and again. Some personalities simply clash. A tree-hugging hippie and a corporate shark may simply be a miss-match.

If one person seems to be making no effort, or barely any, that may be a problem which can't be solved. You have to want a relationship, value it, both parties do. If one party doesn't, they may never. It could be that they can't help it. Some people just can't access that part of themselves. Others are so hurt or simply disinterested. It hardly matters. It could be that they're narcissists and are truly only interested in themselves. You won't be able to change those things, not even with the techniques in this book. It could also be, frankly, that he or she just isn't that into you.

If your partner has an addiction, it may be time to give up and get out. Addictions are red flags of other serious complexes and personality disorders. They create unstable and violent behavior. Addictions can also be addictive, and if you've got addictive inclinations yourself you may be triggered into bad behaviors you've worked hard to avoid. And as with a few other things we've discussed in this chapter, your leaving may be the impetus for your partner to get the professional help he or she may desperately need.

Your partner may fall short of being a narcissist, but he or she may also prioritize themselves above you. Is your time together filled with his or her friends or favorite activities? Are your interests given the short-shrift? You might be able to work this out through clear communication, but it could also be that this partner is subconsciously trying to drive you away and end the relationship in an indirect, passive/aggressive manner. Isn't it better to take a stand and just leave instead of being subverted?

We've talked about how important physical intimacy is to an intimate relationship. And this can evolve, have ebbs and flows. But there some things which just can't be overcome. Some people just aren't attracted to their partners. They try to be, they may convince themselves that they are, but there's a certain chemical attraction between lovers which can't be replaced and cannot be manufactured. One may think they'll get used to the other, but they won't. It's a big part of a downward death spiral of almost any relationship.

There is also the question of sexual taste. Among lovers of any gender or identification, sexuality is a complex part of our lives, both inner and outer. And the spectrum of sexual fetishes is vast and wide and seeming to become more so every day. So, it's really possible that two doms have found each other, that one has a fetish or fantasy that the other simply cannot or will not satisfy. It's possible that one has desires which he or she cannot accept or express. We can't help what we want, as we've seen, only what we do. So, if the other person just can't give us what we want, or we can't give our partners what they want, at least we can all control what we do, and just leave.

Trust issues may just be your undoing. We looked at trust as a red flag for approaching one another with an eye toward clear communication. But even after that, the behavior may continue. If a person is a serial cheater or thief, then they have deep-rooted issues you can't reach and shouldn't be expected to try. Let them deal with it themselves and start practicing some serious self-care.

If your mutual families don't get along, that could also be a serious problem. Forget the grumpy, judgmental mother-in-law of yesterday's sitcoms, it could be a matter of a child who rejects a partner. Or it could be radical cultural differences which make family interaction simply impossible.

It could also be that your partner is a *splitter*, a term for a partner who seeks to separate an individual from their other family and friends. This often happens with people of some money or resource, wherein the partner wants control of those resources. One by one, family members are dopped by the wayside. Their more aggressive attempts are more aggressively rebuked. Lawsuits are filed, power of attorney documents are signed. It happens in a lot of families, and there's really no way to stop it. You can demand that your mother and siblings be allowed back into the house, but splitters are smart and will try to convince you that they're bad for you, that only your partner is truly on your side. Of course, your partner is on one side only; their own. Learn to recognize this situation early on and if you can't stop the pattern from recurring, take what you still have and go … or kick your partner to the curb and give them what they deserve; nothing.

Some of the other behaviors we've mentioned can be more than crisis points but also breaking points; breaches of trust, lack of physical or emotional intimacy, lack of communication.

6

WHERE: RECONSIDERING YOUR ENVIRONMENT

We've already taken a look at how impacting an environment can be on an individual. The environment both reflects and influences the state of mind. It's even more particular with couples, because it's two individuals who would have been used to their own environments. Just as a union is like putting more bumps on the same road, it's like parking two cars in a one-car garage.

We've talked about solutions of being crowded or fighting the feelings of being "suffocated". Private areas, nights out with friends, even separate vacations can be a great way to change the environment in order to affect feelings and behavior. Absence makes the heart grow fonder.

But there's a lot more to it than that.

You may think about a bigger apartment, for instance, if that's how you live. It could be that the environment you share can't be reshaped to make more room. It's a big move, but it could be a good one.

A move together, however, may trigger certain feelings. It's a major turning point, and it may instigate questions and insecurities about the future. One big decision may lead the mind of either partner to consider other options, not ones which will keep the relationship alive. If one partner owns the property and the other, a cohabitant, wants to sell and buy something else, legal complications may enter into it. It may also call into question potentially threatening perspectives of their achievement. It may seem legally invasive too, as if one person is selling out the others small house or condo, let's say, to spend that money in a way that suits themselves. And if you're married householders and genuinely want to stay together but move up to bigger property, you simply may not be able to do so, depending on the economy, the housing market, and interest rates.

Money, am I right?

So, your environment may not be so easy to change as you may wish. Still, it may have a powerful effect on your relationship. If you live in a stressful city, that stress is bound to infect your personal interactions. If your jobs require you to be in the city and you can't just or don't want to head for the suburbs or do a year in Ecuador on the cheap, your options are limited.

Or are they?

One significant question of *where* when it comes to romances is the office or workplace.

Most people under normal circumstances spend a third of their day at work with other people. It's easy to form friendships and even romantic relationships under those circumstances. Human Relations offices in various companies are designed to cope with that common fact.

How can this environment affect your relationship? If your relationship was created at the workplace, it could have all manner of complications. If the relationship goes bad, the crucible of the office will keep proximity tight and tensions high. That disruption could result in job loss, career failure, a downward spiral which could handily result in depression, abuse, ill-health, suicide and death. There could also be legal ramifications, harassment suits and even worse.

There's also the complication if you're otherwise committed, married or in a monogamous relationship, and you begin a third-party flirtation with somebody at the workplace. Even if you don't, jealousies can arise from presuppositions.

Workmates may also take offence to a workplace romance. Promotions may be doubted, other resentments can fester.

Still, these romances do happen and they're not always destructive. But they have to be entered into with caution and reason amidst the heady passion. Here more than anywhere, you have to be aware of the *where*.

But we don't live in the workplace.

What other environments may create romance, either wanted or unwanted?

Family visits are a change of environment which can have a sharp influence on a couple. Going to the house of one relative or another can raise issues of insecurity and defensiveness. Families don't always share the affection that partners do, and things like the Oedipus/Electra complex can be brought right to the surface. Arguments break out under those pressures, and so too do behavior like shutting down.

So, be careful when you're in those environments. Reassure each other that you're there for each other, not for them. Remind the other and yourself that you love each other more than you love the others ... if you do, that is. If you don't, that's a different issue. After all, boyfriends and girlfriends may come and go, but siblings are for a lifetime, that's true. But you don't live with your siblings in your adult years (hopefully) and you may very well live with your romantic partner or spouse (hopefully). Keep that in mind and don't let a three-day change of environment damage a three-year relationship.

Vacations are a big trigger for sexual activity. And that only makes sense, as everything about the marketing of the tourism and hospitality trade is geared toward a romantic ideal. The commercials for cruise ships, resorts, and casinos promise romantic perfection. We're trained to think of big vacations as life-changing indulgences in debauchery (Spring break, anyone?)

People go on romantic vacations sometimes to re-ignite a waning romance, or to find a new romance quickly. But both are illusory, really.

A lot of people hope a romance will save their relationship, but it's rare enough that any deep-rooted issues are going to be resolved on such a trip. They're only being put aside temporarily, and ultimately there's no solution. It's a fool's errand.

And meeting somebody while on vacation can be just as treacherous. You're meeting this person in a world other than their own. As we know, environment influences our behavior. Therefore, if you meet somebody in an alien environment, their behavior will not be the same as it would be in their normal environment, which is likely to be quite different. If a person's behavior is changed in proportion to the difference in their environment, then their normal behavior may be radically different than their behavior in their vacation environment.

As they say, what happens in Vegas... stays in Vegas.

However, there are splendid honeymoons and lovely trips for couples all over the world, and that's great. Travel is an important part of any life, but of a pair of lives in conjunction even more so.

People fall into ruts, it's just a fact. They become bored. And variety is the spice of life. Trips together provide that variety, of place and experience. It can refresh a couple's interest in their world and in each other. Changing the environment may change behavior, it almost certainly will. And these travels may bring out fascinating aspects of one or the other which had gone undiscovered or forgotten.

Date nights are a good way to change the environment to refresh or revitalize a relationship. They lack the escapism of a vacation (which a lot of people just can't afford anyway) but still give two people the chance to interconnect on a personal level. It's a small trip out of the house, a change of scene, a chance to put aside the scramble of the day and be pampered and served just a bit. Recent events have made this an even rarer treat than before, but even under normal circumstances, a nice dinner out and maybe some dancing is a luxury most people overlook to their detriment.

Date nights also have the added benefit of reminding both partners of earlier days, when love was fresh and exciting. One may come to see the other in that old, forgotten light.

Don't forget to dance! Dancing is an erotic exercise. It is liberating, the exercise of a growth mindset which is unconcerned with the judgment of others, Dancing excites both parties, letting go of their inhibitions and letting their instinctive, primal selves take over. It's easier to cast aside the overthinking and negative self-talk when the music drowns it out. In those flashing lights with all those swaying hips and chests on the dancefloor, it's a good way to reconnect on a basic level. And of course, the environment is crucial to the effect.

The same would be true, by the way, in a fancy ballroom, a tango studio, or dancing in a sunny field of daisies. All would be great, actually.

Religion offers couples (and individuals and families too) a new environment which can have tremendous impact on interrelations. Without favoring any particular religion, as there is no need to; the communal and spiritual pursuits of any religious institution can have far-reaching benefits.

We've already mentioned volunteering at a food bank as a good way to increase your self-esteem and to find satisfaction beyond feeding your own desires. Desire to help someone else, right? Well, that brings us to your local church or other institution. This is a way to change your environment in order to change your thoughts and behavior. If you introduce some spirituality into your couple-hood, it could take your focus off your own grievances. There's nothing like hearing about the suffering of others (Jesus, Elijah, Mohammad, the Buddha, Gandhi) to put our own suffering into perspective.

And, as meditation gives us something else to focus on, so too does religion; at least an hour or so per week when you're not thinking about the pressures of the workplace or of the home.

Religions of all sorts also tend to promote the tenants of couple-hood; loyalty and honesty and pure passion, the hallmarks of the ancient family structure of any ancient religion.

First, a word about environment, the *where*. Places of worship, whatever their orientation, are different environments than either our homes or our workplaces or even our recreational centers. They are palatial and ornate, bedecked with stained glass or mosaics. They have a power, a sense of serenity, an empowering and an intimidating presence. And they are designed that way, they always have been. From the Islamic shrine The Dome of the Rock to the Wailing Wall to the Church of Nativity in Bethlehem; from your neighborhood church or synagogue to your local mosque or Buddhist temple, these places are designed to inspire calm and open one's mind and heart to the messages of true transcendence.

Religious institutions also offer support with new friends who are like-minded and who have endured similar challenges. There could be great advantage to enjoying the mentorship of others whose guidance could make all the difference. They're also filled with children and their excitement and youthful glee, always a positive influence on a young couple, married or not.

There are lots of different religious organizations, one to fit every world view. If you're interested in biblical history but too secular-minded to embrace the mystical aspects of biblical lore, that's okay. The wisdom to be found in the two Testaments is well worth knowing, whatever your feelings. If you believe in the Word but have lost faith in the Church and the fallible men and women who run the churches which function in His name, then follow your own path. There is no prescribed path which you must follow. Religion is there for you until you decide that you are there for it.

Whatever your religious perspective, you just may find what you're looking for in simple attendance. At least it will get you to stop thinking about how angry you are at each other, and maybe the reasons why. It's a new and fun activity, if nothing else.

And if you feel uncomfortable with that, which may happen, consider our other previously discussed idea of volunteering. That may put you into other and more temporary interactions with various institutions. Who knows? It may widen your social circle, which may either introduce new and invigorating inspirations that will keep both partners happy, or enlighten each as to the pressures the other is facing. Plus, you'll both have the benefit of having helped others, which is an inspiration which burn internally and which you can take you wherever you go.

And as long as we're talking about *where*, let's take a closer look at places to go, things to do, ways to bring your romance back to life and keep it strong or ways to get that new romance started off right. We've done our homework. Now in the book's second section, let's go out and play!

II

THE HOW, WHAT, AND WHERE OF MAINTANING A STRONG RELATIONSHIP:

HOW TO DO IT, WHAT YOU'RE DOING, AND WHERE IT'LL WORK BEST

7

CLASSES BRING COUPLES CLOSER TOGETHER

You spend a lot of time with your partner. And though you were drawn together by a series of fun mini-adventures known as dates, you've probably settled into a bit of a rut. It's easy enough to let happen, and there are a lot of good reasons for it. Our busy lives are demanding, often requiring two jobs or long gig-economy hours at home. Money's tight, and dating isn't cheap. It's also easy to reason that the courtship phase of the relationship is over, and all that energy naturally goes elsewhere.

But it's crucial to keep your lives amusing. Working too hard and too long has proven effects on physical and mental health. It leads to feeling of burnout, isolation, depression, overthinking, perfectionism, poor diet and sleeping habits, even premature death.

And it's important to amuse yourselves together, embark on activities which will draw and keep you together. So, while separate vacations have their place, it's not in this chapter.

Vacations together can be great too, a classic way to bond and create memories you can treasure. But vacations can also fail you in this effort, so let's take a quick look at that.

You should definitely take vacations together, don't get me wrong. But you can't take a vacation every week, and we're looking for things you can do on a more regular basis. You're lucky to get two weeks a year for a vacation. Also, as we've seen, people aren't quite the same when they're on vacation, and that can be a good thing. It may not be. Vacations can be stressful on a relationship if things go poorly or quarters become too tight. If you're having trouble with your relationship, it's a long shot bet that a vacation will correct those things, unless you're at a couples retreat of some sort.

Let's agree that vacations have their place, but not really in this section. Let's take a look at some things you can do in your day-to-day life, things that will bring you together.

Taking a class together is a great way to spend fun time together and get closer. There are any number of classes available at your local junior college or community center. You may have met your partner in a class of some kind, and that could instigate fond memories. It could remind you of shared interests or inform you of shared interests which you didn't know you shared. You may discover talents you didn't know you had.

Yoga is a great way to spend time together and it has great health benefits. Any exercise class would have the same benefits. There's also the physical charge you'll walk away with, all that testosterone and endorphins which will need release (and at the same time, too).

Meditating together will have a lot of mental and physical benefits, though meditating is a more individual endeavor. Unless you're concentrating solely on each other, meditation may not be perfect choice for a joint activity. It has great benefits though, and doing it together certainly couldn't hurt. It's just not that interactive.

You might think about a martial arts class. That's interactive and steeped in calming philosophies that are bound to inform your personal relationship. You'll each have a practice partner, a support source, and it will give you the same physical rush as a vigorous workout. You'll also get the benefits of all that wisdom and the ability to defend yourself or your partner should it ever be necessary.

Massage classes are an amazing way to spend time together in this manner. It's a joint activity which creates a mutual focus and is physically invigorating. And massage has a benefit few of these other classes, and that's the necessary intimacy involved. You're touching parts of the other's body which most don't ever touch (and may likely never even see). You're touching deep, creating sensations which go straight through the body and into the mind. You are bringing calm and healing. It's practically a type of foreplay (and very often winds up being just that). You'll also learn a lot about the human body, which is a fascinating subject. So, your brain will be excited even as you are a force for relaxation and calm. You'll be able to use your new skills on your family and friends, and you'll be the most popular person in the room. If your boss has a kink in his or her neck, it may even help your career. It's a great thing to practice at home, and think how good it will feel to have all those massages.

You might consider a language class. You'll each have a ready practice partner, and you'll get all the benefits of learning a new language. That excites the brain, sharpens your thought processes, and stimulates the synapses. Learning a second language can be a real career boon too. Being bilingual makes you much more valuable in any number of industries. It could be just what you need for that promotion you've been hoping and working for.

Dance classes are very popular among couples, and for good reason. They include a vigorous workout, they encourage teamwork, they put the dancers' focus on each other. Dance classes can be a lot of fun, and you don't have to be great at it. But you may discover a talent you didn't know you had. Being a good dancer does instill confidence and a certain personal style. Men and women who can dance carry themselves differently.

There are classes for all styles too; tango, flamenco, ballroom, swing, line dancing, modern, tap. Dancing has very sexual overtones too, as hips sway and shoulders roll. It could be just what you need to keep things intimate and frequent.

Some couples enjoy fencing as a hobby. It's physically vigorous, requires hand-eye co-ordination, it pulls the focus of one onto the other. It has the competitive edge of sport the way the others don't, and it's a neat thing to talk about at parties. Tennis, racquetball, even ping pong would have the same positive effects. Tennis may be a bit hard on the joints, but ping pong's pretty harmless. I don't know that you can take ping pong classes the way you can take tennis lessons, but you can still just buy a ping pong table and start playing. It's fun and funny and will give time focused positively on each other.

Art classes are always fun. Painting or drawing are calming activities which, like meditation, draws focus away from the clamor of life. Creative minds are more active. Creativity is one of the signs of a self-actualized person and a growth mindset, which is a key facet of a successful person.

But it's also an activity that you can physically share. Set up your easels next to each other, support each other's work, learn from one another. You're working toward the same goal; you're spending time without fighting or complaining. You may discover a hidden talent or sharpen old skills. If you're handy with a brush or pen, you can show off for your partner, impress them again, the way you did when you met. That alone may be helpful.

Also, painting is a great exercise in goal-setting to achieve an ultimate goal. And you'll have the satisfaction not only of having achieved a goal (painting a painting) but you'll have the satisfaction of having created a piece of artwork. Art has a tremendous positive energy, and so does creating it. Sharing that positive energy can only be good for any relationship.

As long as we're talking about art classes, pottery or sculpture can be a great pastime. The clay is slick and yielding and tactile. You remember the movie *Ghost*, right? If not, go to YouTube and search *ghost pottery* scene and you'll get the picture.

Cooking classes are a fantastic way to spend time together. It requires teamwork, preparation, and creativity. Cooking appeals to all the senses; touching the food, tasting, smelling, hearing the sizzle and crackle, savoring the colors and presentation. It's a great exercise in breaking one big task down into little tasks, each milestone featuring its own small reward on your way to the satisfaction of the final meal.

You also get to eat the meal, which is its own satisfaction. You can happily practice at home, and all that proximity, combined with the sensual delights of the culinary arts, is famously romantic. Countless movies have used a cooking scene to get the characters into bed … or onto the dining room table.

Cooking lessons have other benefits too. Prepared food is cleaner and healthier. You'll lose weight and look better, and that will have physical and mental health benefits. You'll be more confident; people will react more positively to you. You'll be able to control exactly what goes into your food, make sure it's made just the way you like it. Cooking is an important but sadly neglected skill in our fast-food, pre-prepared world.

You can also clean up together afterward, more time to spend together on a common goal.

Acting classes can be a fun way to be together in a positive environment. Acting is a team effort but also a personal accomplishment, and it can be quite exciting. You and your partner can assume different identities, utilizing externalization and other techniques from narrative therapy. It's a good way to abandon your inhibitions. It's a great way to express yourself without feeling vulnerable (once you get over your initial nervousness). And since you're not yourself and they're not precisely your words, you may be able to express the real truths of your life in this way. That's what good fiction is all about.

Improv classes have much the same positive effects and for the same reason. Improv also keeps you thinking on your feet, and that excites the brain and keeps it sharp. It's okay if you're not that great, and you're not alone on the stage so you'll always have support (that's one of the tenants of improv). And improv classes are all over the place, so they won't be hard to find. They won't be expensive either.

Stand-up comedy classes are common too. Unless you're doing a doubles act, you'll be working alone. But if you both do it, you'll be there to support the other, you'll be able to guide each other, work on material together (which you can't do with improv).

You might try a writing class. Writing is also a fairly isolated activity, but it's frequently done by two people. I've collaborated several times with great results. And the practice often strengthened my relationship with my collaborators. Writing is challenging, requires breaking one big task down into smaller milestones, it's a team effort. It's something you can set a timeline for, an activity which can take as long or as short as you can reasonably manage. You can write fiction or non-fiction in any one of countless subgenres. Whatever you enjoy, you can write.

Or you can take the same class but write different projects, each reading the other's for guidance and support. That can sometimes be tricky, giving notes to a writer. But it's a great way to apply some of the communication exercises and techniques you've learned from this book.

Poetry classes are also a superb way to spend time together. Poetry is famously romantic, and for good reason. It can be a fascinating subject; it's filled with history and colorful figures. It's reflective and meditative, and it may allow you to express things in ways you couldn't do before.

Mixology classes are always fun for couples. You'll learn to make all the most popular drinks, which will make you great fun at parties (but watch out you don't get stuck behind the bar). It's a fun thing to practice together, even if you don't drink! They're easy to find and fairly inexpensive, and you don't need a lot of art or sports equipment. But please … mix responsibly.

You might be interested in a home improvement course. Even if you're not a DIY-type in general, it does reconnect a couple with their home, so important for a stable psyche and a happy life. You could pick up skills that save you a lot of money down the line. And you may come out of it with a nice table or spice rack.

Maybe a Kama Sutra class is what you need. The ancient Indian text is a masterpiece on eroticism, sexuality, and emotional fulfillment. The book is famous for its many sexual positions, and that alone could put the kick back in your relationship. Even if you're all good as a couple, things could get even better!

Along these lines, classes on tantric sex are custom-made for lovers. You'll have a (hopefully) ready practice partner, you'll learn amazing things you never thought possible, and you may just wind up a sexual superstar. There are numerous techniques, tricks, and aspects to this ancient school of sexual thought which has only recently become known to the common folks.

Classes are great and have a lot of benefits. But there are other ways too! Let's take a closer look at some other fun activities for couples.

8

PERFECT VACATIONS FOR COUPLES

We went over why vacations weren't the best way to clear up communications in your relationship. But vacations do have their place, as we've seen. And some vacations actually can bring you and your partner closer together instead of simply forestalling your lingering problems. Let's have a look.

First let's visit some of the most romantic cities in the United States, where a lot of us call home. In fact, let's look at the places you actually did call home!

You might consider going to one another's hometown. Meet their old friends, see their old haunts. Share your own! It's bound to give you both insights into the other's past, it may explain a lot about why the problems which have come up are still coming up. And nostalgia is a potent force for positive feelings. Any time you're together and the feeling is positive, it's a good time. Besides, perhaps it's been a while since you've been back, seen the old gang, shown off your awesome partner. What could be better than that?

Maybe Las Vegas, Nevada, which remains one of the world's most glamourous cities. It's packed with fun things to do, places to eat, hotels to visit. It's a place made for couples. The lights and sounds are designed to bedazzle, and the place exudes sexuality at every turn. The showgirls, the pop stars, the place is bound to be a boon to your libido. But don't keep looking too long! Vegas may provide temptations you don't want to have excited. Know your boundaries and your triggers. If gambling is a problem between you, maybe not. Otherwise, you can fly in from anywhere in the country and stay at some of the most luxurious and renowned resorts in the world. It's really quite affordable if you don't gamble, and even more affordable if you gamble really well!

New York City, New York, is also spectacular for lovers. It is steeped in legend and lore, a place where dreams are said to come true. It is the living, breathing personification of the American dream, and it's empowering just to be there.

Sure, the big apple can be intimidating, but it is swarming with great hotels and some of the world's best restaurants. And Manhattan has delights all year around; Spring in Central Park, Christmas on Fifth Avenue, Autumn uptown, summers off the Hudson River. There's really no other American city like it, and it may inspire you to new depths of mutual understanding.

Broadway shows and museums are great ways to spend time together while broadening your horizons. Museums are a great way to spend time together back home too, and though you may not have as many Broadway shows, you've probably got some community theater.

Yosemite National Park in California is gorgeous and secluded, charming and relaxed. If you're a rock climber, another pursuit a lot of couples share, this is the place for you. But for others, there's the amazing wildlife, lush forestry, and of course the big rock face, *El Capitan*. Hiking, skiing, biking, there are all manner of fun couples' activities. It's a photographer's dream, and that's another great way to get closer to one another. Photography is creative and still physical. It's a personal experience but can be easily shared. Each supports the other, the brain and body are activated. The focus is not necessarily on one another, but it's a meditative practice which provides great personal satisfaction. And with digital photography, it's much more affordable than ever before, and you'd be surprised at the results you may come up with.

Wyoming's Yellowstone National Park features over 2 million acres of gorgeous wildlife and the famous geysers Steamboat and Old Faithful. The Lake Yellowstone Hotel & Cabins is the the oldest hotel in any national park and features a stunning view of the lake.

Where else can you take a safari searching for large herds of bison and possible sightings of elk, gray wolves, and pronghorns. Cody, a frontier town, brings you back to a different time, when the town was founded by Buffalo Bill Cody.

Santa Fe, New Mexico may not be on your list of great places, but it's truly great for partners. Not only are the skies and desert landscapes breathtaking, but the town is also an artist's enclave. It is packed with galleries featuring stunning paintings, pottery, sculpture. There are lots of top-notch restaurants and a healthy community theater scene too.

The mysterious spiral staircase of the Chapel Loretto and the Georgia O'Keeffe Museum are not to be missed!

Savannah, Georgia is charming, Spanish moss hanging from the old oak trees, historic town squares and stately mansions. The weather is warm year around, and the restaurants and nightclubs are among the country's best. Forsyth Park, River Street and a walking ghost tour make Savannah a fun and romantic excursion to the American South.

Unlike the more popular islands and cities of Hawaii, Molokai enjoys a slow pace and less touristy feel. Called the friendly isle, Molokai gives any couple time to reconnect in the splendor of the tropics without being crowded with tourists and mega-resorts. Hiking through Halawa Valley, staying at the Hotel Molokai, canoeing, picking flowers for a handmade lei; this is about as romantic as it gets.

With its soaring cliffs, craggy caves, waterfalls, and lush forests, Ohio's Hocking Hills remains among one of the American Midwest's premiere destinations. Old Man's Falls and Ash Cave are highlights of Hocking Hills State Park and are great fun for couples. You can zipline through Hocking Hills tree canopy above Hocking River, repel down cliffs, enjoy the cozy luxury of the Inn & Spa at Cedar Falls.

Snowmass, Colorado is a lovely alternative to the more crowded and touristy Aspen. It's a quaint, small resort town, uncrowded and cozy. With 300 hundred days of sunshine and the balloon festival in the summer is a colorful and fun way to enjoy each other's company.

California's Big Surf has some of the most gorgeous coastal views in the world, with lots of quaint little towns that are perfect for lovers. Julia Pfeiffer Burns State Park features the post photographed waterfall in the *golden state. Treebones Resort* is rustic and gorgeous, and the *Eselan Institute* provides workshops for couples!

San Francisco, California is one of the great romantic cities, with the gorgeous bay, the streetcars, and the famous pier. The delicious crab and incredible hills and the foggy mornings are worth seeing. Key West, Florida, is hot and tropical, with all kinds of boating and fishing and some of the best biking in the whole state. It's steeped in history and lore, famous for legendary figures from Jean Lefitte to Ernest Hemingway.

Historic downtown Charleston in South Carolina offers historic mansions, cobblestone streets, the sweet smell of magnolia in the air. It offers goat yoga classes (yeah, you read that right), the colorful houses of Rainbow Row, and the 500-year-old Angel Oak Tree. Don't forget Shell Island for a fun time searching for sea shells together. They're wonderous and pretty and great souvenirs, and the search is a great way to spend time together.

A trip to Lancaster, Pennsylvania is like stepping back in time and gives any couple a chance to do some shopping for unique furniture, rugs, and famous quilts of the Amish. Their food is rich and hearty, and there are lots of fun activities to forge memories while learning more about one another. You might try apple picking in Maine too, or in any number of states, you'll learn how pies and sauces are made. It's bucolic and seasonal, surrounded by the colors and smells of the changing seasons.

A trip to a vineyard is a great way for a couple to get away from it all. There's lots of wine tasting, fine foods, a lovely environment, and homey surroundings. They're very popular locations for weddings too!

This brings us to the relatively new concept of agro-tourism. This is the notion of vacationing on something like a working farm, for instance. You take part in various things around the place, learning the skills and traditions; be they table-making or tobacco processing. Agro-tourism goes on all over the world, and it may bring you to Israel, Ecuador, Costa Rica, Europe, Africa, all over the world.

And speaking of going all over the world, if you've got a little more money (maybe more than just a little) or if you're cagey about getting good travel bargains, there really are amazingly romantic places to go.

Paris, France is among the most romantic cities in the world. The famous *city of lights* offers one amazing experience after the next. The greatest art museum in the world (The Louvre), incredible sights like Notre Dame, the Arc de Triumph, the Eiffel Tower. The world-class shopping at the Champs-Élysées, the incredible restaurants, the winding cobblestone streets all make Paris a must-see for lovers.

Venice, Italy features the canals and gondola rides which epitomize the romantic pinnacle of Bella Italia. The ancient buildings and incredible food make a trip to Venice an amazing experience which truly cannot be replicated anywhere in the world. Gothic landmarks, St. Mark's Square, and Murano, the glass-blowing region of Venice, guarantee a memorable stay.

Santorini is considered the jewel of the Greek Isles, with white buildings and jagged cliffs and azure waters of the Aegean Sea.

Thailand's Krabi offers incredible blue water, delicious and affordable flood, Thailand has become the playground of the rich and fabulous, with Krabi considered the most romantic of its many beach communities. Krabi is popular among twenty-somethings, which might be perfect for you, or perhaps not so much. But the limestone formations, mangroves, boulders, and a variety of natural wonders will be attractive to anyone. Boating, snorkeling, and five-star resorts make this one of the most romantic destinations around.

South Africa's Sabi Sands Game Reserve gives couples a chance to see a world they could likely only imagine. Find a leopard in a tree or a diamond in the rough, or just rediscover each other, a genuine African safari is a bucket-list item for a lot of people, and seeing all that majestic wildlife in its natural habitat can be a life-changing experience. Surely there is little that gives us a feeling of being intrepid and adventurous. No guns though, please. Take a picture, leave a life.

The Berkshires' Laurel Lake in New England is gorgeous and tranquil, mist clinging to the water. Early winter or even autumn are the best times of the year to be there, when the leaves are bursting with yellow, red, and purple hues. No place in the world is quite like it. Cozy B&B's, big, homey breakfasts with homemade waffles and syrup make this place a snuggler's dream.

In the Indian Ocean, the Maldives is comprised of 26 micro islands clustered together. Swimming, snorkeling, boating, surfing, amazing views and spectacular beaches, it's one of the most beautiful and desired honeymoon spots in the world. When you go, make sure to spend the day in Male, the capital, to walk the main street, Majeedhee Magu.

Maui, Hawaii, is much better-known than the Maldives, and a bit more crowded. But it features amazing sites and lots of things for couples to enjoy, including Kaanapali Beach, the Hana Highway, and Haleakala National Park, The Pools at 'Ohe'o (aka the Seven Sacred Pools).

Italy's Amalfi Coast overlooks the Tyrrhenian Sea, sharp cliffs and mountainside villas make this such a breathtaking region. Moderate climate makes it a great destination year-around, and the fishing villages and beaches are almost as welcoming and nourishing as the Italian people themselves.

Back in the United States, Aspen, Colorado has long been the winter jewel of the jet set, the ski town extraordinaire. Those gorgeous mountains and resorts have earned every bit of its reputation. The quaint downtown area features unique restaurants, boutiques, and even an opera house from 1889. And nothing beats on outdoor hot tub with your partner, especially in the snowy winter!

Santiago, Chile, might not have jumped to your mind when thinking about romantic getaways, but that's part of what makes it so special. Though it's not nearly the only thing. The

Neptune Fountain at Cerro Santa Lucía, the view of the Andes Mountain range, a big city, the Chilean coast. The incredible Plaza de Armas to the Metropolitan Cathedral is a one-of-kind experience. You can hike in the summer and ski in the winter.

While we're in South America, Quito in Ecuador is the gateway to the Amazon Rainforest, a must-see for anyone. Lush jungles, rivers teaming with piranha and snakes and caimen, exotic birds and monkeys in the trees. The indigenous people are welcoming and share the knowledge and wisdom of their traditions. Bathe under a waterfall, enjoy amazing local fruits and meats. It's one vacation which is certain to last in the hearts and minds of any couple. And it's so gorgeous and memorable, it really has to be shared.

This brings us to actual couples' retreats, combinations of vacations and therapy. Here are few of the better ones.

The Northampton Center for Couples Therapy (NCCT) boasts a fully licensed, on-site team which is dedicated to couples counseling. It's the only one in the US which does. It's known for a variety of restoration methods, including Brent Atkinson's PEX-T model Gottman Method to Emotionally Focused Therapy.

It's not cheap, but it's important to keep in mind that none of these places are. But if it's the right move for you, it may be worth the investment. All of these retreats run a few thousand dollars a day or more, and that may or may not include travel. It's part counseling and part romantic vacation.

Sedona Soul Adventures in Sedona, Arizona is as much about counseling as it is about renewal and revival in a spiritual and customizable experience.

Mexico, Texas, Utah, and California offer Life Marriage Retreats. The principles of perspective, commitment, forgiveness, accountability, and trust. They're designed for marriages in crisis and offer a hands-on approach over a four-day retreat.

Sonoma, California offers the Healing Couples Retreats for a blend of hands-on coaching and research-based interventions. They offer a shared group retreat and one-on-one private counseling.

Beautiful North Carolina offer the Marriage Rescue in Huntersville, a Christian-centered counseling retreat. It offers 3- or 4-day retreats and six months of telephone support to follow up. Their programs are completely private, which is what many couples prefer.

Kokomo, Indiana's Relationship Rescue Academy works couples through an incredible six-month course in an even-more amazing three days and all sessions are completely private.

The famous Marriage Boot Camp is as much for unmarried couples as married couples, perfect for preparing and educating the partners for marriage. It also services married couples in crisis.

Make sure to avoid retreats which embrace a neutral stance. You're not going there for a neutral stance. You need help and you're paying for it. Find a practice which will avoid hot-button issues. It's not about fighting, it's about *not* fighting, right?

Your marriage retreat of choice should respect your personal boundaries. Select a retreat that honors your personal goals for your relationship. You don't want to get caught up in a cookie-cutter approach, and that can be common among retreats which don't have private sessions and even some that do. You are individuals and as a couple you are unique, and you should make sure whatever retreat you select understands that.

Make sure the approaches are tested by research. There are a lot of fly-by-night retreats that will take your money and give you nothing but a lot of hot air. You'll want a place with a hands-on approach.

Try to choose a place that will offer practical follow-up care. You may have great success at your retreat, but the weeks and months that follow will be crucial. Without follow-up you may backslide into your old habits and lose all the ground you've gained together.

Now that we've looked over vacations and retreats, let's take that closer look at things you can do around your neighborhood. They're not as committal as a class and not as intense as a vacation or a retreat. They include all kinds of fun things which are perfect for couples, in crisis or not.

9

FUN ACTIVITIES TO KEEP THE RELATIONSHIP FRESH

The important thing is to keep your communications open and your relationship alive. Prevention is worth a pound of cure, they say. So, it's vital to keep life enjoyable on a continuous basis. It's important because it's all too easy to allow the negative things to build up; the time pressures, the self-doubt, the lingering resentments. And with our busy schedules, recreational things like things we're going to look at are often the first things to go by the wayside. A lot of us have so many responsibilities to others that we neglect the responsibilities we have to ourselves. But we have to be conscious and conscientious about how we spend our hours, our days, our weeks.

And if you've found yourself with some problems which have been gathering, these are good ways to get closer and clear up those communication breakdowns. They're basically all very affordable, creative, and are proven to work. They can be done repeatedly, in combination, and you definitely shouldn't stop at just one. Check 'em out!

You might think about having a no-tech day. You'd be surprised how much tech dominates your life. Between your smartphone, your computer, the television, screens are everywhere. And with the internet, there are endless distractions to come between you and your partner. Also, all that unnatural light is bad for your eyes, sitting at a computer for too long can give you a blood clot, and watching too much television can cause depression, lethargy, weight-gain, poor sleeping habits. So, shut it down for a day. And it's not like you have to go to an amusement park as an alternative. Have a house-cleaning day, another great thing to do as a couple as we've seen. Enjoy the quiet of the house. Have some small talk. Take walk outside, do some gardening. Read a book to one another, that will give your partner a chance to hear your voice in a positive context, wrapped around exciting words of romance or adventure. It enjoins you both on a fictive adventure without ever leaving the house. Or just take a nap; anything other than high tech. You'll feel refreshed, trust me, plus your house will be clean.

Making plans for your future is a nice way to get closer, because the whole nature of it is based on the idea that you're both still committed. It's also a great way to engage the Pomodoro method of breaking up a big goal into smaller, attainable steps. Those little victories will boost your confidence as a couple, just as they would in an individual pursuit or as when a team is involved. You might be saving for your wedding, for example, which means making a time table and a schedule, making deposits into the savings account together, researching locations. It's fun and constructive and keeps the two walking down the same path in the same direction.

A couple's massage is a great idea, like a mini-mini-vacation. You'll lay together and be pampered, savor the sensuality of a deep-tissue backrub, luxuriate in a mud bath side by side. It's relaxing and rejuvenating and refreshing. It's more than a date, and what more is that it's time you're spending together which is guaranteed to be positive time and leave you both feeling great. That's what you need to achieve and maintain clear communication and keep that hidden negativity away.

Going on a double date is always fun, and something we may find ourselves doing less and less. It's nice to see friends again, and to watch our partners connecting with others. Bonding with others helps a couple bond with one another. Other people may bring out things in your partner you've forgotten about; a little laugh, the turn of a shoulder, a surprisingly quick wit. Their flawed romance, seen objectively, may just look more fondly on their own relationship, which they see subjectively.

Stargazing may sound like an old-fashioned way to spend an evening, and it is. Perhaps this is so because our cities and towns are increasingly big and brightly lit, which blanches out the starlight from below. But there's always the rooftop, or a quiet hillside spot somewhere outside of town. Check the internet for a good spot. But it's really relaxing and romantic. Since mankind first looked up, he was gazing into the stars. It's the birthplace of all philosophy, and astronomy is the father of all sciences. Nothing can make a person quite so reflective as looking up at the stars. And when there's a meteor shower or something like a blood moon, it's a truly spectacular sight.

Along these lines, watching the sunset together is also a calming and bonding experience, and one you get to do every day if you like! There's oftentimes nothing more breathtaking than a beautiful sunset, all those colors streaked across the sky, changing right before your very eyes. It's almost meditative, and it's an experience you share with your partner.

Some couples write live letters to each other. It may sound corny, but it's potently romantic. And let's face it, there are some things that are just harder to say. Writing them down still gets them out, and it gives them additional power. Those words can be read and re-read, sinking in deeper each time. They're lovely keepsakes too, and could be powerful reminders of your love in times of conflict or crisis.

Or you could play naked Twister. I know, it also sounds corny, but like couples' game night it's good, clean fun. Well, maybe not so clean, but you may not realize that when the game originally came out it was lambasted by some conservative groups as being overtly sexual.

Unless you really swing, you might want to leave Twister on the shelf for couples' game night. But this is a great way to bond with friends and with one another. You get all the benefits of a double date while getting the stimulation of a couples' activity. Charades or other participation games of the sort (like Pictionary) are always great, and a quick search on the internet will handily deliver plenty of these to get you through the evening. Trivia-based games are perfect for couples' game night, as are murder mystery role play games.

Binge-watching a new series or having a movie marathon is always fun. That's a day lying around in bed or on the couch, comfort foods and cocktails, all the comforts of home. There is tons of content out there. But choose that content wisely. Classics and romances and sultry thrillers may all be good choices, but avoid argument dramas like *Who's Afraid of Virginia Woolf?*

Some couples like to make a scrapbook, which is a fun and endearing way to spend time together. It's creative, keeps the focus on one another, and helps you visualize your relationship, which gives it its own special power. This scrapbook, like your love letters, may come in handy later when doubts and suspicions come creeping up. A few nostalgic moments with the scrapbook could be just what you or your partner needs to be reminded of what's so right about the relationship.

Then have sex in every room of your house. Not all in the same day, necessarily (but it's something to think about). But you might make it a personal challenge to do the entire house over the course of a given month (February, perhaps). Don't tell your partner either, just let it happen. After one particularly romantic meal in the dining room, throw the dishes off the table and have at it. One night after doing the dishes, do it up against the fridge. The living room's easy to wrangle, and the shower is right there in the bathroom. Just do it. The spontaneity is bound to thrill, the change of environment has a big impact on the act (as we've seen) and you'll be certain to obliterate any sexual rut you may have fallen into.

Singing a karaoke duet is great fun, something couples do all the time. You can go up there and clumsily shamble *Summer Nights* or *Islands in the Stream* or *Up Where We Belong*, or you can really practice it at home and blow your friends and coworkers out of the water. It's a fun practice activity, because you can do it around the house, as you cook or clean. Just download a karaoke track from the internet, pop it into your smartphone, and play it anywhere. You may be a better singer than you think. Karaoke is a good couple's activity anyway. One person is there to support the other, it's expressive and there's no pressure. There's liquor too, if that's your thing, and often these bars serve food. It's like a date and game night and a musical performance all in one.

A lot of couples sext each other. This, of course, is dirty talk over a text line. Imagine sitting in a boardroom meeting or a lecture class to be interrupted with a naughty suggestion from your partner, and you return it right there and then. There's a certain voyeuristic appeal to it, it's a dirty little secret. How much fun is that? Some people send naked pictures, often very close up, of particular parts of the body, but we can't recommend that. The pics may come back to haunt you or your partner. Doesn't mean it isn't hot as hell, it is; we just can't recommend it.

Make a logo which represents your couple-hood and leave it on little notes or when you sign your love letters. It might be a combination of your first initials. My brother Eric and his wife Christine have one, a lowercase *c* which curls into a lowercase *e*. They wear theirs as a small tattoo which each of them has. I recommend Post-It notes for now, but hey, you do you.

Creating a new tradition is good, because it's predicated on the idea that you're both in it for the long haul, that you're building a future together. You might take any of these fun activities and do them on a regular basis and boom, it's a tradition. Sunday singalongs? Tradition. Game night first Saturday of the month? Tradition. It gives you something to look forward to, a goal to achieve together.

Silly though it may seem, playing a round of mini-golf is a fantastic way to reconnect and stay reconnected. There's no pressure, like karaoke, the worse you are at it, the more fun you can have. It's colorful and amusing and cheap, and it can really bring you back to earlier days, frivolous and childish, beyond the pressures and stresses of the world.

Some bars will have trivia night instead of karaoke, and that's great too. Everybody plays with every question, it has teamwork and pits your wits against the others, bringing you together. You'll learn a lot and you may even know more than you realize. If you've got a head full of facts, this is a great way to remind your partner how smart you are!

We mentioned amusement parks, and those are perfect for reconnecting. Chances are, you went to at least one amusement park when you were dating, and going again will bring back a taste of that honeymoon period. The rides are exhilarating, the whole experience is engaging in every way. Your brains are excited by the colors and figures and shapes surround you. All is cheerful, you're surrounded by smiling children and proud parents, which can only help you visualize your own future. If there's a Ferris Wheel, take it and then kiss at the top. It's a moment for a picture postcard. If you're lucky enough to have fireworks going off in the background, you're in heaven.

Bowling is a great recreation for couples. It's a physical activity, mutually supportive but individual at the same time. It's slightly competitive. It allows time to sit and chat and eat and drink. And there are usually pool tables nearby, another fun couples' activity.

Bingo is fantastic for couples. You play as a team against the others, so it's a bonding experience. It's mentally engaging without being too challenging. There's a competitive aspect, the thrill and rush of gambling and sometimes even winning! You may find it at your local bowling alley, actually, with automated systems on big television screens.

Riding a horse on the beach is great if you've got a beach nearby. That's something straight out of a romance novel, and it's like a tropical getaway that's really no farther than your nearest beach. If you haven't got one, a ride through the desert is just as spectacular in its own way.

Taking a spontaneous road trip is a great little getaway. I know we've already mentioned vacations, but these are more like weekend getaways. The key is to do them in the spur of the moment. Or you may do a little planning first and then just come up with it on the spur of the moment (as far as your partner knows). Either way, think about getting in the car and heading off. A road trip is fun and adventurous, and there are lots of B&Bs and places to stay, just for a change of environment and a change of pace. It's the spontaneity which give it its punch.

Go to a rock concert or big show. Make it a glamorous night, with a nice dinner and fine dress. Have a night at the theater, a play or a symphony, or the opera. Or rock it out with Paul McCartney next time he comes to town. A big show is a special thing, that makes it a special night, and that makes each member of the couple feel special, it makes the *couple* special.

Have sex in some exotic place. We're not suggesting you break any laws, of course. But an erotic night in someplace like Las Vegas has its own allure. One aspect of this is the famous Mile High Club. To join this exclusive number, you have to have sex in a plane (and that's all you have to do). Generally, a couple will each go into a certain lavatory separately, have sex, then step out one at a time. I suppose others may charter a plane just to fly around while they have sex in the main cabin. Either way, this isn't the most economical excursion, but it could be well worth it. And really, a flight from Burbank in Los Angeles to Las Vegas is only a hundred bucks round-trip, so that's two sessions for two hundred bucks, not much more than a hotel room. And you can have a meal in Vegas before flying back, refreshing yourself and replacing your electrolytes.

You might try making love while you bungee jump, but I'm not sure I can recommend that. However, the big B is popular among couples. It's something you do together, it's invigorating, and the rush it creates is bound to be powerfully impactful on both partners.

Handsome cabs are a charming way to reconnect and stay close. A horse pulls you through Central Park or some comparable place, the conversation flows as the sites drift past. It's like stepping into a different era, one of charm and romance.

Camping is always a fun time, and there are campgrounds near almost every big city or suburb. Getting back to nature is refreshing, a drastic change of environment. The quiet of the woods or the desert or the sea, the crackle of a fire, the way the food tastes. If you're near to a hot spring, that's its own big boon. It will leave you empowered in ways you've never imagined, that I can tell you.

Speaking of that, while you're at home, spend some time cuddling up by the fireplace. Fire is mesmerizing, it's warm and colorful and comforting. What's more romantic than cocoa by the fire, or a nice snifter of warm brandy, or a hot buttered rum, curled up and snuggling. It invokes a sense of heart and hearth; home, family, love.

Have you ever thought about recreating your first date? You can work it out ahead of time and surprise your partner with it. Take him or her to the same place, eat the same things, go to the same movie theater or come home to watch the same movie you saw together that first time. The power of the nostalgia will be amazing, but it will also show how much you remember that first night, how much you think about your partner and your relationship, how valuable it all is for you. That will make it, and you, more important to your partner.

Doing a jigsaw puzzle can be fun. It's an open-ended pursuit, you can't really time-log it. But you can spend a lot of time together working toward a shared goal. And you'll have the satisfaction of having finished it and having done so together. And you'll have a cool picture worthy of framing. It will serve as a reminder of what you can do when you work side-by-side, creating a thing of beauty despite the many little challenges.

And of course, there's the classic breakfast in bed. Surprise your partner by getting up early, present all the colors and shapes and smells of a hot breakfast lovingly prepared and presented. And make enough for yourself so you can climb in and enjoy it too. All of these activities are for both to share, after all. And speaking of activities which are for both to share, let's get into the next chapter. Do you really need me to say it?

10

SEX AND COMMUNICATION AND HOW TO BRING IT ALL TOGETHER

We've already established how important sex is to an intimate relationship. It is the most intimate expression of our thoughts and desires, it reflects everything that we are and very often everything that we hide. It's often memorable, though not always for the right reasons. It's the manifestation of our drive to reproduce. It's at the very core of our beings in our fears and desires. It reverberates through our organs and blood and genitals. It's on our very surface, in our skin and hair and clothes, faces and fashions. It's in everything we see and everything we're sold. It's the measure of our success and failure, beyond the mere money and power. We're obsessed with it because we're trained to be.

People between 18 and 29 years old have the most sex according to recent studies, having sex roughly 112 times per year, or roughly two times a week. After 30, the number seems to drop to around 86 times per year. After 40, it's just under 70 times. But that doesn't mean you don't want to have it, whatever age you are. Because let's face it, when it's great, it's *great*.

And no book about relationships would be complete without a look at sex. But there have been volumes written on the subject. There are volumes on the psychology of sex, the underpinnings of certain fetishes, ways to introduce those things into your lives. So, there's no real reason to discuss the psychological subtext of bondage or role play fetishes or any of them. That's a different book for a different time.

But there are some things which are independent of whatever you or your couple may or may not be doing. They're not about getting to the bottom of why you like what you like. As we've seen, you can't really control what you like, only what you do. So, if you enjoy wearing a red clown nose, have at it.

What we're talking about here is a way to approach sex which centers on communication between couples. After all, clown nose or nurse's uniform or what have you, sex can often become a very isolated and isolating experience. Despite being as physically close as two people can be, despite being closer emotionally than with essentially any other, we're often little more than two people slapping against each other in the dark. Even in that most intimate moment, we're often alone in our own thoughts, our own world. We close our eyes, we retract, interacting only physically.

So, let's take a look at some of the practices we can take into the bedroom which rely on and accentuate clear communication. You may also be about to learn the most potent sexual techniques you will ever know.

DIRTY TALK

Probably the clearest and most basic form of sexual communication is dirty talk. It can take the form of sexting, as we've seen, or phone sex, which was quite popular only a few years ago and there's no reason it shouldn't be even more popular now with the ubiquitous nature of smartphones in our lives. Facetiming is probably the future of that practice, but hey, whatever brings and keeps people together is a good thing.

But we're looking at dirty talk in person. It entails hearing the voice, your partner's and your own. It's about giving power to your feelings by speaking them. It's about the strength that wells up with language you wouldn't use otherwise. Because the first thing you should know is that dirty talk is *dirty*. It's not loud, it's not mean, but it's not polite either. But in dirty talk, you're abandoning civility, you're throwing your inhibitions away. You're communicating your deepest desires, your truest self; you're declaring, in your way you're demanding.

And because that language is so anti-social, it carries with it the thrill of rebellion, of wildness. When you speak that way, you're not speaking as you're civilized self, and you're not speaking to your partner's civilized self. You're speaking to each other the way only you two could. If a waiter or coworker threw some dirty talk at your wife, you'd be furious and (hopefully) so would she. But this is a private thing, like sex itself, something you reserve just for the other.

It also has a tendency to bring out the most primal aspects of our nature, that part which rejects the norms of society and be willing to do anything, anywhere.

I know what I said.

Next, dirty talk doesn't have to be restricted to the bedroom. Next time you're at your couples' game night or even at your partner's parents' house, try siding up to him or her, leaning in and whispering something like, "I want to ___ you so hard right now, take you in the bathroom right here and now." Then just walk away. Because you're not demanding that you do it, just putting the thought in their imagination. Then your partner will be thinking about it too; they won't be able to think of anything else! They may just pull you aside and make that happen, though you'll probably be as quiet as you can in that instance. Still, that repression of sound, that lack of communication, is a powerful thrill all its own.

But let's go inside the bedroom. Nothing is as powerful as dirty talk in the bedroom. This is true because we so often retract into our own worlds. Men may be doing math or employing other techniques to maintain their stamina, a woman may be trying to well up an orgasm practically on her own.

Let's also take a minute to discuss what dirty talk is not. It's perfectly healthy to tell your partner what you want, and what you want may be dirty, but that's not dirty talk. It's okay to guide a lover to where and when and how hard, and that's closer. But it's still to civil, too practical. Dirty talk is animalistic, primal.

Say how beautiful your partner is while you're engaged, in any stage of your lovemaking. Tell them what parts you like best, say those words with extra zeal and relish. Remember, these are not things you say to everybody all the time, and words have meaning. Search for and find all the meaning you can just in the way you enunciate the word. It also matters where you say it, close to the ear. It's intimate in every sense, that means being close. Part of dirty talk is how your voice resonates in your partner's body, that's what makes it such a potent form of communication.

And remember that they're beautiful in the dirtiest sense. Use the dichotomy of words like *beauty* and *gorgeous* with the sharp frankness of the expletives you'll use. The contrast will be mind-spinning, I assure you.

Let that primal beast in you rise to the surface. You're climbing to the pinnacle of ecstasy, not ordering a steak dinner.

You can actually control your own and your partner's performance by using dirty talk. Escalate your voice as the passion escalates. Increase the tenor of your demands. Insist upon interaction, don't let dirty talk go one way. Ask a rhetorical question, one about your mutual satisfaction, and demand an answer. Then demand it louder. Just the act of speaking, of hearing one's own voice, is empowering and creates a connection between the two of you during what might be an isolating exercise. Instead, it only brings you closer together.

VERBAL FANTASIES

Before we get to the more complex communication-based techniques (just be patient) it's time to talk about the communication-based fantasies. How do they differ from non-communication-based fantasies? Beyond simply dirty talk, these fantasies require communication in order to take their proper effect. For example, a threesome is a popular fantasy for a lot of couples and individuals alike, but it doesn't require any real communication, just three willing people. Likewise, a bondage fantasy may require no communication at all (just consent).

The soul mate fantasy, on the other hand, hinges on communicating, on speaking. Here, the dirty talk isn't used merely to excite and flatter, but you're taking a subtle kind of control over your lover's mind. And that's powerful communication.

The soul mate fantasy is simple. You're already using your dirty talking skills to drive them into a physical and mental state of ecstasy. But then you turn your dirty talk away from the superficial and toward the soulful. You're not going backward into the romantic, that's not what I mean. You've already flattered and engaged them. Now is the time to tell them that you're meant to be together, that you fell in love with him or her the moment you saw them (or whenever that was, there's no need to lie). Say that you're soulmates, that you'll always be soulmates. Make sure you get an answer and one in the affirmative. It will only really work when they respond in the affirmative. Just as you have to say it in order for the other to believe it, your partner must say it in order for him or her to believe it.

Same thing for the pregnancy fantasy. In this fantasy, you're building toward creating a pregnancy. As you make love, you cajole your love to admit that they desire to have a child with you (you can do this even if you're the female partner). You work them up, tell them how much they need it, demand they answer you. If they deny it, challenge them, assert your growing personal power.

Tell them that you can feel that it's going to happen, you can feel all that energy building up in both of you, new life ready to explode. Tell your partner how great the child will be, how perfect a childhood, that this young life will go on to save the whole world! Tell your partner that they're the only person who could make it happen, that your pairing is the only magical one which can create this life.

Give it power by giving it words, by giving voice to it. That will be infectious and it will carry from one to the other and then back again. Your partner may even take over the experience, but once you've taken control you should hold onto it. It doesn't matter where you are physically, above or below, in front or behind. The center of the power is squarely between the two lovers.

But be careful with both of these techniques. When you can control what a person is saying, you can control what a person is thinking. And these two fantasies in particular reach down to the center of a person's psyche, two of a person's most primal desires; to be loved and to procreate. So do not engage in these fantasizes lightly. You'll get a terrific result to be sure, but you could also be making subconscious promises which you'll be consciously held to keeping. Anyway, it's manipulative if you don't mean it. Clear communication is open, honest communication. Lying is the exact opposite.

A variant on these fantasies is the virgin fantasy, wherein one pretends to be a virgin and the other extols the virtues of initiating their partner's journey into sexuality. From here we slip into slutty schoolgirl fantasies, weird incest-things, and other matters I'd just as soon leave to some other writer of some other book. Either way, there's little denying the powerful influence of verbal communication in sexual intercourse. And we're only really just getting to the good stuff.

VERBAL EXERCISES

Unlike verbal fantasies, verbal exercises are more intense, deeper, resonating far beyond any fantasy, as potent as they are. But these verbal exercises can be truly life-changing. This is as close as we come to the tantric models of sexual self-control, and this is only a brief visit to a subject you may want to deal with in greater detail. But in terms of sex and communication, you're about to set into the final frontier.

The first verbal fantasy is known as the *orgasm on demand*. It's a bombshell for women who've never had an orgasm, and this may just be the key. Because when you can control their language you can control their behavior, you can control their bodies, and then do what they cannot do for themselves or what others cannot do for them. And when you can do that, you've used communication to secure your relationship, instead of to destroy it.

Observe:

You're making love, slowly ramping up the energy and the passion. You're using dirty talk in order to excite your partner's primal, anti-social instincts. Your partner is answering in the affirmative, and the energy is increasing.

Now, instead of turning your attention to a fantasy, turn your attentions toward that orgasm. Tell your partner that you know they're thinking about it, that they want it. Promise them that they'll have it if they trust you. Demand their trust and promise an orgasm. Demand that they acquiesce. Now draw their attention to different parts of their body, tell them to feel their legs, their arms, always accentuating those parts of the body in your dirty talk ("Feel those long, pretty legs, feel that heart pounding in your chest …"). Draw them from every part of their body until you've focused their attention on their genitals, the orgasm which will be lurking beneath it.

Tell them it's there, but they just have to find it. Demand that they do. If they can't demand they try harder. It doesn't matter, as you'll encourage them to feel it growing, feel it rising up and soon enough they *will* find that. Tell them they can feel it growing inside them, that you call feel it getting bigger, even if they can't feel it yet, you know it's there.

Keep the physicality of your intercourse strong, getting steadily stronger if possible. Tell them that you can feel it coming on strong, encourage as much as you can. Keep your partner encouraged to drive that orgasm higher, higher, telling them it's getting bigger and bigger. It will.

Then refuse them. Change course. Keep up the physicality, but tell her (or him) that you won't let them have that orgasm. Absolutely forbid it with every bit as much command as you used before.

Command that they refuse themselves, deny themselves even as your body works harder to make it impossible to refuse.

Note how crucial the act of communication is here, and how particular it is to intimate couples.

The contradiction between the physical inspiration and the verbal refusal will have your partner's head spinning around. Do not let them have that orgasm, whatever you do. Tell them to wait, to forestall it as long as they can even while you do everything you can to bring that orgasm to life.

Then make them beg for it. Make them beg for you to allow them this simple, natural expression. Because you've taken control of their body, their mind, their will. Demand that they beg and they will. Now, instead of being unable to have an orgasm, they're almost unable *not* to have one.

Almost.

Because you deny them. You refuse them until they beg louder and you go on driving your partner's body over the point of no return. They'll beg until they're screaming for release.

That's the time you grant it. In fact, you demand that they have an orgasm. It's happening anyway, so you retain control and make yourself the cause. Demand that they absolutely explode! Use all your dirty talk, the dirtier the better. This is a moment of blinding lack of reason, of pure primal instinct. It's the least social moment of your week, so make it that times a thousand.

You'll produce that orgasm, and if you don't keep going until you do. It will come in the denial phase. If it takes one or two tries, so much the better. Practice makes perfect!

A variation of this exercise is known as the *countdown to ecstasy* or sometimes *the 10 count to orgasm*.

Take yourself back to your dirty talk. Once you're both excited and you direct your attention toward that orgasm, you build up just a little bit, but don't go off the rails, because what's going to happen is carefully calculated.

Begin a nice, slow pace and let your whispered but commanding voice begin to explain that you're going to count down from 10, and when you get to one, your partner will have an orgasm. Remember you've got ten counts to go, so start off nice and slow and give yourself room to build.

Pause on each number, don't rush from one to another, but pick up the pace just a little bit with each descending number. And linger on every number, stay on nine for a good long while before counting down to eight and cranking things up just a little more.

Sprinkle in lots of dirty talk between counts, flattery and aggressive lust. You're in control. Don't be afraid to get creative: *"Seven now, angel, sexy seven ..."*

Keep increasing the base at a very incremental rate. Your partner will be likely to be focusing inward at this time, measuring their bodies and waiting for that one. Don't let them. Demand that they open their eyes and look right at you. It's an amazing power move, and it will keep your partner directly engaged and focused as much on you as on themselves.

Count down slow even as you ramp up the pace. It's the contrast of the frenzied action and the elongated suspense which will excite the psyche. You'll be getting closer to the final count, but you'll be getting to them more slowly, stretching out the time even as you deliver a frenzied pace.

They'll start to beg as you withhold the four, the three, the two…

Then taunt your partner, as for them to beg for it, demand that they do. They will, they'll shout out the number for themselves.

Deny them.

Go back to ten and start again. It's important because, like the orgasm on command, you assume control of your partner's orgasm. In this way, you become the only person who can control their orgasm, or give them one at all. They'll associate you as being the gatekeeper of their own bodies, their souls, their lives.

And why? Effective communication in an intimate relationship, just what this book is all about… life, too.

But sometimes your best efforts aren't good enough. Something more is wrong, nothing is working. Why, and what do you do next? The next section of the book will answer those questions and more. But it's a lot less fun than reading about visiting Ecuador.

III

THE HOW, WHAT, WHY, WHEN, AND WHERE OF COMMUNICATING IN A BREAKUP

11

THE ELEPHANTS IN THE ROOM

There are some things which can challenge a relationship and can be dealt with in a number of ways. It only seems right that we take a look at them here. They go a bit deeper into darker territory, things which may well spell the end of your relationship.

ERECTILE DYSFUNCTION

The old phrase refers to the subject everyone is aware of but which nobody wants to talk about. But if things just aren't going right, if all the tricks and techniques are still coming up with one of two predictable outcomes, it's time to just take a frank look at them both with frankness and honesty.

A lot of men suffer from erectile disfunction, or *impotence*. Some ED is common from time to time, especially in times of distress.

Occasional ED isn't uncommon. Many men experience it during times of stress. If it happens chronically, though, it could be a sign of significant health problems which have predictable remedies. It could also be rooted in psychological or emotional problems. Let's take a look at the easiest ones first.

An erection is what happens when blood flows into your penis. When it doesn't, you haven't got an erection, you've got a problem.

The most common physical causes include diabetes, high blood pressure, cardiovascular disease, high cholesterol, kidney disease, obesity, stress, age, low testosterone or imbalances of the hormones, anxiety, relationship problems, and depression.

Other known culprits include medications for depression or high blood pressure, sleep disorders, substance abuse, certain diseases such as Parkinson's or multiple sclerosis (MS). Pevronie's disease (scar tissue in the penis) or pelvic damage may have the same ill-effects. So will certain prescription medications, such as those used to treat high blood pressure or depression.

ED can be caused by only one of these factors or by several of them. That's why it's important to work with your doctor so that they can rule out or treat any underlying medical conditions. Learn more about the causes of ED.

Treatment will depend on the cause; it may require medication, change of diet, or therapy.

Some common pharmaceutical treatments for ED include sildenafil (Viagra), vardenafil (Levitra, Staxyn), and avanafil (Stendra), and alprostadil (Caverject, Edex, MUSE). Low levels of testosterone may require testosterone therapy (TRT).

If you're interested in the so-called *talking cure*, or *talking therapy*, you might look into a number of programs designed for this very problem. You'll be looking into anxiety, stress, post-traumatic stress disorder (PTSD), and depression. Expect to talk about feelings about your sexual well-being and be ready to visualize what it is you really want.

Symptoms of erectile disfunction include trouble getting or maintaining an erection, reduced interest in sex, premature or delayed ejaculation, inability to achieve orgasm (anorgasmia).

Of course, the causes may be psychological rather than physiological. A person facing the psychological aspects of ED may be prepared to answer questions such as the following. Ask yourself:

How often, per month, do you have sex and has this changed recently? How firm are your erections, and why? What contributing factors are there? Do you have erections in the middle of the night or in the morning?

What is the state of your relationship? Happy and sexually active? Are there any changes in that recently? Are you currently under a lot of stress?

Are you currently taking medications or using tobacco, alcohol, or illicit drugs? Are there any underlying conditions, such as a heart condition or diabetes or pelvic injuries?

Other diagnostic tests may include ultrasound to test blood flow, a nocturnal penile tumescence (NPT) test, injection tests, urine and blood tests.

Kegel exercises may be helpful and not nearly as invasive. Just identify your pelvic floor muscles. Do this by stop peeing while in midstream. You'll feel those muscles at work that's your pelvic floor. Now contract them for three seconds at a time. Do that 20 times in a cluster, three times a day. Kegels may be easier to do lying down at first, then try it sitting or standing up. It could be as simple as that. Guaranteed it will strengthen your muscular core in any case.

Around three hours of weekly exercise for roughly six months could also lead to a decrease in erectile problems! Boom, price of admission yet again!

Diet can reduce inflammation and constriction of blood flow, to allow more blood circulation to the penis. Fruits, vegetables, whole grains are all good. Red meats, processed sugars and full-fat dairy are to be avoided. Alcohol should only be used in moderation.

Herbs and supplements for ED include asparagus racemosus, dehydroepiandrosterone (DHEA), ginseng, L-arginine & L-carnitine, and yohimbe. Zinc and horny goat weed may also help. Talk to your doctor before taking any supplements or drastically changing your diet or exercise regimen. Some of these supplements, like yohimbe, may have dangerous side effects.

Some people use acupuncture to cure ED, but *I* wouldn't want to try it!

Much more attractive seems prostatic massage, which is a form of massage therapy. It couldn't be much worse, right?

Studies indicate that about 30 million American men have erectile disfunction, and it only increases with age. With each decade, the average of ED sufferers increases by 10%. But it happens among a lot of younger men too, largely for different reasons.

True, ED does tend to increase as a man gets older, but there are ways of dealing with that, such as a more nutritional diet and more exercise. Testosterone is the natural inspiration for an erection, and the body creates it simply by requiring it. It's needed to propel the body through physical activity. So, get some exercise and your body will create the fuel it needs for that exercise and for other exercises as well.

There are lots of medications and treatments available, but you might be well-advised to avoid them. Pills can have all kinds of side effects and some devices (pumps and implants) can have terrible results which cannot be remedied.

ED can be traced back to several common conditions, and controlling it could be a lot easier than you think. Here are the best tips and tricks to prevent or reverse erectile disfunction.

First of all, try to keep any medical conditions like diabetes and heart disease under control. Get regular exercise and maintain a healthy weight. In your weight regulation, focus on a healthy diet and not on binge fasting. Manage or reduce stress in your life and keep a close eye on feelings of depression or anxiety.

If you smoke cigarettes, stop doing that. It's bad for every aspect of your body and mind and is especially detrimental to proper erectile function. Excessive use of alcohol can have the same reaction. And keep in mind that different body chemistries react differently to different alcoholic influences. Same for drugs which aren't prescribed by your doctor (and even some that are). Some things just work against you in the end, if you understand my point.

FEMALE ORGASMIC DYSFUNCTION

Women, on the other hand, may be more apt to suffer from orgasmic dysfunction, the difficulty of achieving orgasm even with sufficient arousal. The condition affects between 11% and 41% of surveyed women in recent studies.

Women may have difficulty reaching orgasm due to contributing emotional, physical, or psychological factors may include medical conditions like diabetes, advanced aging, surgeries, or use of certain medications, especially selective serotonin reuptake inhibitors (SSRIs), which are taken for depression.

Studies found that religious or cultural beliefs, guilt, shyness, history of sexual abuse, depression or anxiety, lack of trust, stress, low self-esteem or unresolved relationship issues were most often to blame. A combination of these factors could also be likely.

Though the principal symptom is the inability to achieve an orgasm, other symptoms include unsatisfying orgasms or a prolonged period before orgasm. Even masturbation may not correct the issue.

There are actually four separate types of orgasmic dysfunction. In *primary anorgasmia,* you've never had an orgasm. *Secondary anorgasmia* is difficulty reaching a climax, even though it wouldn't be your first. The most common type is *situational anorgasmia,* when you are only orgasmic under particular situations, such as in a public place or during masturbation. The inability to climax under any circumstances, no matter how high the level of arousal or sexual stimulation, is called *general anorgasmia.*

During a scheduled doctor's appointment, you may be asked to consider a variety of questions, including questions about your sexual history. But that can be helpful, so trust your doctor and don't be shy.

Treatment will depend on the underlying cause, ranging from medication to the talking cure, depending. Couples counseling is a popular way to deal with this particular condition, and can touch on other parallel concerns at the same time. These conditions do often come in clusters.

Some people use hormone therapy, including estrogen and testosterone therapies. We recommend more organic remedies, if possible. There are over-the-counter supplements and arousal oils such as Zestra, which warm the clitoris and vastly increase stimulation. Oils such as these may be more than useful for masturbation and intercourse as well. Be careful about any interactions which might occur with anything else you're taking or using.

KINKS, PARAPHILIAS AND PARAPHILIAC DISORDER

A *kink* can be defined as a non-conventional sexual concept, practice, or fantasy.

Paraphilias is defined as intense sexual arousal by atypical situations, objects, or fantasies. Those who are turned on by sweaty socks, food, particularly strange roleplay fantasies are often-cited examples.

When that interest impairs a person's life, or someone else's. it's considered a *paraphilic disorder.*

Kinks are very common and most experts agree that they're generally perfectly healthy. You can't really explain them and you don't need to. Just about everybody has a fetish of some sort. And the days when these fetishes were considered anti-social or otherwise outside of the mainstream are gone.

You don't need somebody who shares your fetish, but you'd want a partner who'd be willing to try just as you'd be willing to try theirs, right? If you do find someone who shares your fetish, all the better. There are plenty of online sites for that, but always be careful on the internet.

Fetishes can be a central part of many healthy relationships. And a lot of couples try new fetishes that neither had enjoyed before. That's a good way to keep the relationship lively and it should give you something to talk about.

But it can be difficult to express your desire for such an experiment. A person is often bashful and embarrassed. That's what an intimate partner is there for, right? To listen actively without blame and judgement. So be open and welcoming and give it a fair hearing. If you're the one asking, don't be negative about it, or even bashful. Proclaim, declare, it could be a fetish which has always been of interest to your partner and they were also reticent to mention it. Make sure you are self-accepting and self-sympathetic. If you're not, your partner may not be either.

And while we're talking about declaring, if you want to try something in the bedroom, don't ask. Don't force it on anyone or do it unannounced, of course. But think about verbalizing it as a statement ("I want to try …") instead of a request ("Can we try …?") They can be resistant, but they can't refuse because you didn't ask. It's a way to retain power, and in this conversation, you may need all you can get. In fact, research indicates that couples who indulge in kinks also tend to communicate better outside the bedroom.

In the case of paraphilias, it may take more than trying it once. If you really don't like what they really do like, perhaps even need, that's something to seriously consider. You can't change it.

A recent Canadian illustrated that the fascination for particular behaviors is much broader than previously known. Over 35% of people surveyed, for example, were turned on by voyeurism, 26 % by fetishism in general. Almost 25% of the subjects studied enjoyed frotteurism (the rubbing of one's genitals up against someone without their knowledge or consent. Just under that same amount were fascinated with masochism, or self-suffering, and that proclivity was equally spread among men as among women.

Exhibitionism proved very popular, as did urophilia, when urine is arousing. Vorarephilia is the desire to be eaten by another being, and diaperism is the fascination of dressing like, acting like, and being treated like a baby.

It could be a gradual change from kink to disorder. It could be easy enough, for example, to enjoying bondage (a kink) to doing it all the time and need it to enjoy sex (paraphilia) to the point where it affects other parts of one's life (paraphilic disorder).

Diaperism and other age-related fantasies, can quickly dominate a person's life and become disorders. Grown women enjoy acting like infants, little girls, sassy tweens, can also become debilitating. This is because it's more than just a sexual act, but a lifestyle commitment which can affect other parts of their lives. Imagine a guy who likes to put on a leather mask and whip his partner. If he likes it, it's a kink. If he needs it, it's paraphilia. If he wears the mask to the grocery store, it's a paraphilic disorder.

But it's not so cut and dried. Some people are addicted to sex, and they do it with compulsion. These people are apt to shut over people and things out of their lives, limiting opportunities. And if you're partnered with somebody who has a paraphilic disorder, you're either in or your out.

Research indicates that paraphilias cannot be changed. But they can be understood and managed. Some use therapy, some use sex-drive reducing medication. Paraphilic disorders cannot be treated, and most who have them don't want treatment. Most are perfectly happy with their lifestyles. And nobody has a right to judge or change it. You won't be able to and you shouldn't try.

GYMNOPHOBIA

The crippling fear of nudity is a condition called gymnophobia. It certainly ranks among crippling bedroom maladies, one where things get real... or so unreal that it may just be beyond your reach.

Gymnophobia often results from a traumatic experience, a form of post-traumatic stress disorder (PTSD). Sufferers of eating disorders and body dysmorphic disorder, a fixation on a person's own bodily imperfections, often suffer from gymnophobia.

Some people who are afraid of being naked suffer from eating disorders or body dysmorphic disorder, a mental condition where people believe they are ugly or fat or imperfect when there is little truth to it. People with this disorder often obsess over their appearance, hiding their bodies from themselves or others. Others could simply feel they do not measure up to media images of beautiful bodies and feel nervous about showing off their bodies.

Also, people with extreme forms of anxiety and obsessive-compulsive disorder (OCD) can sometimes feel uncomfortable about being naked in front of other people, due to the intrusive, compulsive thoughts that accompany the condition. Sufferers of extreme obsessive-compulsive disorder (OCD) and anxiety often suffer from this phobia.

Experts generally treat this nudity phobia as they would other phobias, encouraging gradual, safe, controlled exposure to the subject of their fear. A patient with this phobia might be encouraged to wear less and less when in the safety of the home, gradually working toward their goal.

These and other maladies could be the last line of defense. If these can't be overcome, if nothing you've tried in this book has worked out, it may be time to face the end. Let's take a look at the *how, when* and *where*, of that.

12

WHY, WHEN, WHAT, AND HOW TO END IT GRACEFULLY

You've tried everything, but the problems go on and they may even be getting worse. In that sad case, it may be time to face the facts. Not every pairing is a good one. Sometimes people really are incompatible. One or both of you may have problems which require serious treatment outside of a couple situation. It could simply be a matter of selection, not rejection. But it's important to understand this event as clearly as you can so you can handle it and yourself in the best manner possible.

Breakups can be rough, there's no doubt, sometimes very rough. So, you owe it to yourself and your partner to handle the event with grace and calm. Nobody wants to be the one who freaks out when the end comes. Nobody wants to endure that kind of emotional baggage or walk away miserable.

And, as is the beginning and the body of the relationship is key. Unfortunately, communication hasn't helped you in this case, but you can still do your best.

The first thing to avoid is self-blame. If you've used the techniques in this book, then you've done a lot more than most. You've certainly done all you can do (unless you're not being completely honest with yourself, but that's on you). But being left by an intimate partner can easily leave a person feeling doubtful, insecure, consumed by negative self-talk, and overthinking. And this can be crippling. A person may spend days, weeks, months, even years wondering what they could have said or shouldn't have said, what might have been if only they were more of this or less of that. A person may become fixed-minded and project a pattern of rejection into the future, be fatalistically certain that they're doomed to rejection. One may be prone to think they've lost their last, best chance at happiness.

This creates a downward spiral of career stagnation or even career loss, further self-loathing reinforced by the continued failure it inspires. Opportunities missed create more overthinking and the anxiety that goes along with it.

The effects of this can be crippling, even deadly, as they commonly lead to depression, poor sleeping habits and diet, substance abuse, and suicide.

It's vital to avoid this. There will be some unfortunate emotion involved, yes. And it's important not to suppress that emotion. Emotions are like food; you need them to survive. They're nourishing and necessary. But you can't carry them around forever. They have to be processed and the waste product expunged or else they will fester and become toxic and eventually they will corrode you from within. So be prepared to deal with the emotions and with the reason. But like a lot of what we've been talking about, it comes down to the *hows*, the *where*, and the *when* of how to do it.

WHEN YOU KNOW, YOU GOT TO GO

The first thing to consider is that breaking up is not always a bad thing. It's not good for anybody to waste time, energy, and money in a bad relationship. Relationships are meant to support us, make us feel more whole, more satisfied. Their place in the hierarchy of needs is fairly low, just above the basic needs. But if they're failing us, if they're preventing our self-actualization instead of helping us work toward it, then that's a good situation to get out of. In fact, being trapped in a bad relationship will prevent you from moving further up the hierarchy.

A lot of people fear being single. Autophobia is the actual fear of being alone in a room, but we're talking about people who don't want to live alone, or to die alone. But it's important to remember that the relationship which is ending is not the last relationship you'll have. Being single frees you up to be available to meet that new person, to go to new places and pursue new activities. Take another look at the things this book recommends for couples, and they'd all be great methods for individuals. Volunteer at a food bank, take some lessons or a class, take a spontaneous excursion.

Being single also gives you time to focus on yourself. Instead of thinking about what your partner is thinking or feeling, wanting or desiring, you can turn that focus on yourself. Be careful not to overthink or fall into negative self-talk, of course. Practice self-sympathy. If you can't help your partner, you can still help yourself.

As we agreed, some pairings just aren't good ones. But how do you know when the time has come to cut it loose? You don't want to be premature and live with doubts about whether you could have made it work if you'd only stuck it out a bit more. When do you know you've been hanging around too long?

Hanging around too long is a problem too. A lot of people may forestall leaving the other until after Christmas. But that mercy Christmas will ring sour in their memory, and it's not likely to be a very happy holiday either. They'll only wind up being miserable on Valentine's Day in six weeks anyway.

A lot of people say that there are *breakup seasons*, window of time that are better or worse for the breakup. They'd say Christmas is off-season, but the window opens just after the new year. It's open season on broken hearts until late October, when the holidays come around again. Nobody wants to be responsible for somebody's holiday suicide.

In truth, there's no good time of year to do it, so I'd say ignore all that. But there are signs you won't miss.

One of the big signs that it's time to end a relationship is that you're not acting like yourself. You might be more emotional or timid or withdrawn around your partner? That's not good. You won't be able to keep doing that, it's not healthy, and it's not honest. It's the exact opposite of clear communication, that's for sure.

Look for things like tiptoeing around or hiding things, over-monitoring yourself in your partner's company, feeling anxious and frustrated in your partner's company, worrying about being judged, avoiding eye contact, being dishonest or less than honest or if there are trust issues that just won't go away. If there are just basic differences in world views, social or political perhaps. These are deep-rooted perspectives which aren't likely to change and can be the cause of unending conflict.

If your partner is putting you down, ridiculing or humiliating you, it's time to go. That kind of abuse will only get worse, and nobody deserves that. These can be back-handed statements, sly little digs, or full-on bellowing diatribes. Enough is, at one point, enough.

And don't be fooled by the contrition which may follow. Contrition is a part of the abuse cycle; it does not reverse it, it furthers it.

We've mentioned hiding from your partner, that's bad. But it's no better when you're hiding them from your loved ones. If you're pulling back from them, it could be for any number of worrisome reasons. You might be depressed, a common reason for withdrawal. You might be ashamed at the way your partner treats you. You could be ashamed that you haven't mustered the courage to leave that person yet. Your partner may be a splitter, working to separate you one by one from your friends and family. We've looked at this and it's a treacherous play. If you're with a splitter and you've tried to correct this practice without success, it may well be time to end things.

Speaking of your family and friends, they don't like your partner, and I mean really don't like them, it might be time to reconsider. If you've been together this long and nobody's warmed up to him or her, it could be that they're seeing something from an objective viewpoint which you are missing in your subjective position. By all means don't let this be your only deciding factor, as it's your relationship and not theirs. But give it fair consideration, especially if there are other things on this list at play.

You may find that your own behavior is the problem, not theirs. And the nature of this particular behavior can be tricky. We've looked at abuses your partner may be heaping upon you, but you have to ask yourself if you haven't slipped into some abuse behaviors yourself. And it may be particular to one particular person, this particular person. If they appear weak and you have a domineering manner, you may find yourself getting frustrated and angry. And while this is a problem you should be able to solve, you may also have to admit that there are two sides to every compatibility coin, and you might not be the shiny side as much as you think. And maybe the other things about your partner may be right about you. You may simply be not that into your partner as much as you were at first or hoped you'd be. So, you may be self-sabotaging the relationship to prompt an end without having to put it quite that way.

For some newer relationships, one partner or the other may feel things are moving too quicky. Does one partner talk about marriage too soon, introduce the parents too quickly? Is one person too instantly reliant and clingy? The feelings which inspire these behaviors really should be parallel between the two partners, and if one is way off track of the other, it may be a sign that this relationship just isn't going to work out. The two are likely to react that way to virtually everything in life. It also means one may be unrealistic in their outlook, and that is a certain way to be disappointed. It may also mean the other is emotionally withdrawn and will consistently hold back and be resistant to the other's love. Through neither's fault, the failure of such a relationship seems certain.

If you're having relationship anxiety way too often, it may be time. At a certain point, you're not moving forward, you're just going around in circles. How do you know when you're at that point? Ask yourself if you're constantly questioning their behavior when they're not around. Do you suspect them of cheating or gambling or drinking? Do you seriously doubt their love for you? If you do, there could well be a reason, there probably is; and I'll bet you already know what that is. Do you constantly doubt your own value and what you're offering the relationship? Your partner may have broken down your self-image, or you may have withdrawn so deep that you know you're functionally dead in the relationship. There may be no coming back from that. Something caused the abuse or the withdrawal and those things are probably beyond your grasp by this time, at least in this context.

Along these lines, if you keep breaking up and then getting back together or taking little breaks, it's probably time to call it. There's a reason that keeps breaking you up, probably a family of related reasons. It could be insecurity, maybe a touch of autophobia, which keeps driving you back into each other's arms. Or it could be laziness or boredom or a fixed mindset, overthinking or negative self-talk. But no healthy relationship has ever been born of these things.

If you keep telling yourself things will get better, they probably won't. Time is precious and it's foolish to waste it with false hope or delusion. It's even harmful be caught in such a cycle, both mentally and physically.

If you constantly find yourself fantasizing about other partners, that's a problem. That's your subconscious mind telling you that you crave something else, perhaps not something better but certainly something other. And you may notice your partner lost in thought more and more, eyes wandering to attractive strangers or even friends and coworkers. Sometimes it's just a pretty face, but sometimes what you're looking at is the writing on the wall.

We talked about one person being too clingy too soon, but being too clingy at all can be a real problem. First of all, any couple should be the result of equal amounts of contribution. A couple is a union of strong individuals, but clingy people lack a certain personal strength. One shouldn't be relying on the other for company every minute, for constant emotional support. It' a sign of emotional stuntedness and it can create jealousy, paranoia, resentment, overthinking, negative self-talk, and can lead the sufferer into more dangerous conditions and complexes. It's a warning sign that you'll notice early on, and you may be best to avoid if you can't put a change to it quickly.

If you've lost trust, because they've cheated on you, stolen from you, or lied to you, think about ending it quick and clean. A person who behaves this way probably doesn't share your priorities at their core, and you'll never be able to make a good relationship with somebody like that. Even if they have other good qualities, and they're bound to. They'll do it again because they don't see the activity as intrinsically wrong. They may even blame you, for falling short or being fool enough. Do they even care that they hurt you, or do they simply hope to smooth things over until the next transgression? The cycle of abuse applies here, to an abuse of trust; friendly, angry, abuse, contrite. And without trust, there can't be any real love.

If you or your partner has been generally unhappy with the relationship of marriage for an extended period, years perhaps, think about calling it quits. Life is short, as we have found.

Sometimes lives diverge in different directions. New career moves may pull a partner one way. One may want children, the other not. People grow through their experiences, and they sometimes do grow in different directions until they're really nowhere near each other anymore.

So, there are real reasons a relationship may simply be doomed to the trash heap of your romantic history. But before you take the crucial steps and sit your partner down, take a moment to reconsider that not every breakup is mandated. There are times, in fact, when you want to sidestep the obvious trap of a breakup, which may seem more obvious at some times than at others. There are common situations which cause premature breakups, so beware.

There are lots of other ways you'll know your relationship is on its last legs.

If you're too agreeable, that can be a problem. You'd think the opposite, but easy agreement is often just another way of tuning out, not caring even enough to disagree. If this has been your pattern for a long time, give it some serious consideration as being symptomatic of a communication breakdown. If you can't reconnect, it's a communication crisis.

If your partner isn't the first person you share good news with, watch out! This is your most intimate relationship. You rely on and are there for your partner more than anyone else. If you're not sharing your triumphs and failures with them first, it means they're not uppermost in your mind. If you call your mother or your buddy first, that speaks to your priorities. Don't be willfully ignorant. Also, imagine how your partner would feel if they're not the first to know about that pregnancy or promotion. It can be seen as a betrayal of trust, and in a way, it is.

If you find yourself repeating things over and over, that means your partner isn't listening. If you've tried to get to the bottom of that (through the techniques in this book, for example) and failed, it may be time to cut loose. If they're not listening, it could be that they either don't want to know, are ignoring you, or that they've just tuned you out. None of those are acceptable for a long-term relationship.

If either of you refuses therapy, that's a bad sign. Even if they don't think it's necessary, if one of them does then it probably is. And a caring partner would go just in aid of the other. Refusal to do so represents a fixed mindset, somebody who is probably more fearful of judgment as a failure than they are in the final results of the sum efforts. It's not such a big sacrifice, and either partner could yet learn something valuable about themselves.

If you're staying out more often and avoid spending time at home with your partner, that's a big problem. Home is where you're supposed to feel most comfortable. You'll never be happy if you dread going home. Never.

Feelings of isolation and withdrawal are harmful, as we've seen. If you just can't beat them, it's probably because you're not with the right person. Does your behavior change around others? If so, reconsider who you're with. You owe it to yourself to consider it, at least.

If you've got kids and you spend more time with them, that's a problem. It's not to say you should put your partner above your kids, of course not. But you're not having an intimate relationship with your kids, so different rules apply. And you might be spending more time with the kids subconsciously as a way to spend less time with your partner, and that's really the problem.

The song used to say, "It's in his kiss." If the love is gone, your partner's kisses will tell you. A kiss is a very intimate expression, and it reveals much about a person's passion or lack thereof. Even a desire to kiss or an unwillingness to kiss can be very revealing about the mindset of the person behind those lips. When the kisses lose their heat, if one partner refuses to kiss at all or does it only with some begrudging quickness, that says a lot... maybe too much.

Weight gain is a bad sign. It's symptomatic of overeating and substance abuse, bad sleeping and exercise habits. It can create depression which only feeds the cycle of misuse and increase the weight gain. This creates a downward spiral we've seen in this book before, and the results are devastating mental and physical health results which often result in premature death or suicide.

When all one partner sees (or mentions) is the other's negative qualities and none of the positive ones, perhaps they're only seeing what they want to see. If so, it's to reinforce what they want to believe, what they've already decided and only need to confirm; that the relationship is doomed.

If you've stopped talking about the future, that's a sign that one or both of the partners just aren't thinking about a future with the other anymore. In that case, there may not be one.

Hair loss is a glaring sign of anxiety and stress, and it usually comes with a very severe cause like marital distress. Don't mistake this for male pattern baldness and mistakenly blame your partner for this, though.

If you spend more time with your friends than your partner, or more time in a group than with the two of you alone, that's a big red flag. It means you're ignoring each other, and if you're still doing that after trying everything in this book, you might be through.

Digestive distress is a common sign of stress and anxiety. It could be that your gut is telling you something. Only you can answer that for sure.

BAD REASONS FOR BREAKING UP

Petty irritations are no reason to break up. Those can be dealt with. If the techniques in this book haven't helped, there are others which may. But petty annoyances are bound to pop up in any relationship, and if you don't learn to deal with them then you'll just be running from one relationship to the next.

If you're just generally happy, think first about the other things which may be making you unhappy. Ask yourself what would make you happy instead. Ask yourself a few if/then questions, reconsider what it feels like to be happy, visualize that, externalize it. It may not be the partnership which is the problem.

That usually does the trick to reignite the relationship and have some fun.

Another reason to break up is if your core principles are vastly different, or if your lives are going in different directions, but don't let the fact that you have different interests break you up. Learn about and partake in the other's interests, as you would do a couples' game night or an art class. That's something you can do together, and it just may broaden your horizons.

Even if you're both attracted to other people, that's not necessarily a reason to break up. I don't mean being attracted to all other people, or many other people, that's a problem. But a lot of healthy couple have so-called cheat lists, people each would allow the other to sleep with under certain conditions. Famous celebrities are often at the top of the list, people both partners know aren't going to wind up anywhere near them. Still, they're attracted, and that's okay if you don't let it come against you or between you.

Don't leave somebody over money, unless they're stealing from you (or spending you into the poorhouse). Money is a principle catalyst for breakups, and you're likely to have these problems with any partner you have.

Don't leave just because the honeymoon phase is over. That's when the real loving *begins*, not ends! Little annoyances you hadn't noticed earlier may rise to the fore, but they can be dealt with using any number of the techniques used in this book.

Along these lines, don't leave somebody because your partner isn't fulfilling your every dream. Your childhood dreams were probably a bit unrealistic to begin with. Unrealistic expectations are the basic building block of disappointment. And this is reality, not the dreamworld. You may not be fulfilling every lofty expectation either, but it doesn't mean you're not a good partner or worth keeping.

Don't let fear of commitment keep you from further committing if that's what feels right. Fear of commitment will keep you running from one person to another for the rest of your life if you don't deal with it. And you could be missing out on great relationships in the doing.

But if it has to be, it has to be. The best thing is to accept it, learn from it, conduct yourself in a way which reflects the best you. Leave yourself with nothing to regret. You may even learn a lot about yourself if you handle the breakup right, and walk away feeling empowered and not depressed, growth-minded instead of fixed. So, let's look at how to break up with someone without destroying yourself physically, mentally, and emotionally.

BREAKING UP IS HARD TO DO

It's something a lot of people dread and probably rightfully so. It happens to everybody at some point, and yet we just don't know how to communicate during this often-traumatic event. Granted, it isn't always traumatic. Sometimes two people just agree it's time to give up the ghost.

Now that we've looked at *when*, let's look at *how*.

Breakups are as unique as the relationships they're ending, so the best we can do is lean on our new understanding and apply what we know. If you apply just a few of these tactics you're bound to have a smoother breakup and a smoother and shorter recovery as well.

Of course, there are a lot of variable factors to consider. Which end of the breakup are you on, the instigating or the receiving end? It's a lot different for the dumpee than the dumper, if you will, but each has a lot to think about when navigating these treacherous waters. Is the relationship turbulent, or have things been quiet before a final eruption?

Other questions have for forward-looking ramifications. Do you want to remain friends? Do you share a workplace or some other vortex which forces you together? How do you get over it, and what one wants to get back together? Which one that is will make a big difference.

So, let's get to the nuts and bolts of getting through a breakup.

HOW TO BREAK UP GRACEFULLY

Always do it in person. To dump somebody by email or, worse, text or message, is cowardly. You were there for the relationship, you should be there for the breakup. Also, only then can you offer the human touch that an email or other method, even a phone message, can't offer.

Be graceful. No matter which side of the breakup you're on, it's not easy. But it's harder for the person being broken up with. If that's not you, remember to begin with everything you like about your partner and don't be blameful. If you're the one being dumped, do not lose your temper or have an emotional outburst. You'll want to, but it won't help. You'll feel a lot better about yourself later if you remain calm and reasonable and then have your emotional freak-out in private.

Remember that the brain cannot be both emotional and rational at the same time. This is a time for reason, not emotion. So, fight it with all your might and maintain your dignity. It will impress your soon-to-be-ex-partner. And who knows? The future may take a turn, some people do get back together. Don't do or say anything now you may regret later (and you will).

If you happen to be in public during a breakup (which you should never be) then heed these words even more so. Throwing a fit in a public place isn't good for anyone, and it will only prove to your partner that he or she is making the right choice.

Along these lines, do not become destructive of the person's things, start throwing things into a pile in the front yard in a heap of spite and revenge. This isn't communication, it's lashing out. It's a violation of trust, because this person trusted you to not to destroy his or her things. It can have all kinds of legal ramifications, and it will obliterate any chance of getting back together. Even if that's nowhere near your intentions now, you never know. And it's just pointless destruction that will prove that you're not a good partner for your ex (or probably for anyone). Then go get serious help with your temper control issues.

While you're communicating during a breakup, try not to make the other person feel better. It's counterintuitive, because guilt and some shame will make you want to comfort your partner. It's no longer your emotional responsibility on one hand, on the other it may only make them feel worse about losing you, since you're suddenly so loving and supportive. And they'll resent later that you reserved all your grace and kindness for the end, once it was too late and it was of no use. You're showing them the best of what you are just as you deprive them of that.

Resist a final session of intercourse too, that will only complicate things emotionally and make the person feel manipulated and used, and that's probably the case. If you're not willing to just cut it off, rethink what you're doing and why you're doing it. It only forestalls the ultimate replay of the breakup scene anyway, and it'll only get worse every time.

Immediately after a breakup, you should cut ties respectfully, at least for a time. Give both parties time to adjust, to accept that it's over.

Contact may give false hope and prevent a partner from healing and moving on.

The problem is that you likely had a strong friendship with this person, though obviously not strong enough. Or other issues prevent the friendship from moving forward. Either way, you've sacrificed some of that friendship for the intimacy, and when that was lost some of if not all of that friendship may be forfeit. You can't ask somebody to remain a close friend with a broken heart and then have them watch you connect with other people. That's selfish and egotistical and hurtful to the other person. It's hard to say goodbye to one of your best friends, but that is what you're doing here. Know that.

Get advice before you do it, a friend of yours and not of your partners. That may be seen as going behind their back. You've got friends of your own, get advice from them. Then remember it when you're sitting down with your partner.

Recognize that it's a matter of incompatibility and resist blaming or shaming.

Do it quickly if you can. Don't let it drag on for hours, with the other partner begging or trying to convince you to change your mind. If you're going through with this, your mind's made up. You're not there for more constructive couples work or even therapy, you've (hopefully) tried all that. Now, just get it done. Don't be rude or frank or cold, of course, be respectful of what the other person is feeling. But you don't have to feel it with them, and you don't have to endure it. If they're getting emotional, cut it off. Advise them to calm down and to sit down again once they're rational and not emotional.

Be truthful; not blameful, truthful. The reality is more than either one of you as individuals, because the relationship was more than either of you as individuals. Recognize that, externalize the problems from the people.

Stay positive about your time together, but don't go overboard with it or you're likely to inspire an argument, a contest to your logic. And that makes sense. If the relationship was all that great, why are you ending it? Just be kind and don't let the partner feel worthless or to blame.

Don't ask for time to reconsider, because that will only forestall the inevitable. You've already given each other time to reconsider, you've been considering this yourself for some time if you're the one initiating it. But your partner may beguile and confuse you. Time to reconsider is only wasted time. And trust has already been damaged. The other partner will always be wondering how close you are to doing it again, what they're still doing wrong. They're likely to be defensive, withdrawn, inhibited. Along the same lines, you don't need a break, two weeks apart. You've probably already tried that and it didn't work. Besides, what you probably mean to say is you'd rather table the issue until it becomes moot. If you want a break, you probably have your next relationship in sight or already lined up. It may already have begun. True, it's a lot more convenient to come back two weeks later and explain you fell in love with someone else, rather than admit you were with them for weeks before the break. Things change, and isn't that convenient. Even if there's nobody else, you're probably hoping there would be, while you're letting your partner spend their energy hoping for something that's not going to happen. Your gambit may pay off, but it's more likely that it won't. Then what kind of scene will you be having, and whose fault will that be?

Just make it clear that it's over and try to move on. It won't be easy, it won't be pretty, or it wouldn't be ending. But sometimes it just has to be done.

WHERE TO DO THE DEED

Never do it in public. Some people feel this is a good way to make sure the other person doesn't throw a fit. But that's not true. They may still do that, and feel even worse that you lured them into that kind of trap. People know that gambit and they'll feel manipulated. If you fear for your safety, that will only forestall a violent confrontation later. Do it in private. If you live together, have a plan to leave them in peace for a while afterward to digest the news. Be careful though, because if they're going to trash your stuff or steal from you, this is what's going to happen.

Never do it at a family event, as this would be terrifically humiliating. Some people may reason that they have their family nearby for comfort, but that comes at a terrible price. And you'll find yourself a pariah.

This being said, sometimes a public place like a park or the beach may not be terrible ideas. They will curtail a person's possibly anti-social behavior, and that could be a concern. It could be that you'd feel more comfortable out of doors, where the tension between you won't collect in some small room. Feelings of claustrophobia can take a person in times of emotional crisis, and the ocean breeze is always a calming influence.

Another benefit to being out of doors and in public is that you probably met there. That means you can always walk away and then drive away. You're not leaving your possibly enraged partner in a house full of your valuable and vulnerable things. You're not in danger and you can control the situation.

If you live alone, do you want the person in your home or apartment? You can always ask them to leave, and it does put you in your place of comfort and power. But it also puts your partner at a severe disadvantage, lacking the home advantage. And what if they won't leave?

Meeting at their place gives them the comfort they may need, and you can always simply walk away to leave them to digest what's happened. But being in their place of power may empower them, and if they're in an emotional state, things may become more emotional.

A word about abusive people. If you're breaking up with them, you might want to take other steps. If you were or are in an abusive relationship, you were probably (hopefully) in therapy. Abusive relationships require that, if they have any hope of survival (not to mention the people *in* the relationship). So, consider meeting at your therapists and breaking up there. Your therapist will be there to moderate and ensure a peaceful resolution, if one is possible.

If you share spirituality in your relationship, a session with your spiritual leader or guide could be helpful too. These could be good approaches even outside of abusive relationships, if you're particularly worried about the emotional tumult which might ensue.

13

THE HOW, WHEN, AND WHERE OF MOVING ON FROM A BREAKUP

It wasn't easy for either one of you. But it's over now and you're going to have to deal with it and get on with your life. Hopefully, you're a growth-minded person who is ready to accept failure as a steppingstone to success. But getting dumped can rob you of that essential ability to see the positivity in certain situations and in life in general. And that creates downward spirals which may take you to the lowest times in your life, or even to the end of it.

So, the steps you take at this time will make all the difference, especially if you're the aggrieved party. Let's face it, it's a lot easier for the person doing the dumping to move on. In a lot of ways and in some very concrete instances, they may already have done so. You must do the same, to process the emotion and then let it go and move on with your life.

Still, that's a lot easier said than done.

WHEN TO KNOW IT'S TIME TO MOVE ON

Emotions will come first, as we're about to see. Then, before you apply the techniques below, you'll want to be certain that it's not just another bump in the road. Your partner could change their mind, right? *Right?*

You'll know when the time is right to get back on the horse. But keep these things in mind. Do you really want a new relationship, or to get back to the previous one? Are you ready to take the risk? Have you really left your ex behind? You don't want to bring any residual ill-will from that relationship into the new one. And you don't want a rebound, that's not fair to anybody.

But you don't want to sit around forever either. You have to push yourself beyond your comfort zone, you have to put yourself out there. Changing your behavior will have an affect on how you think and can reverse a downward spiral.

It's different for every person in every situation, so the only real advice would be to know yourself, be in touch with your feelings, and avoid the traps of overthinking, negative self-talk, isolation, substance abuse, and depression.

It's up to you!

WHAT TO DO AFTER A BREAKUP

The first thing that will result from the breakup will be the emotional fallout. Hopefully you didn't let it out during the breakup, you kept your cool and remained reasonable and rational. But you're bound to have emotions about it and you must process these emotions before you can do anything else.

A good way is to just cry it out. Have a few drinks if you need to (be very careful here) and then just let it all pour out. Nothing wrong with doing this alone. Remember that this is emotion, not reason. So, you don't need a friend to be logical with you or to talk you around. That may work once you're a bit more reasonable, but the first thing you have to do is expunge the emotion. Do it big, do it quick, and keep it up until there's no more left. Leave as little residual emotion behind to clog up your system.

Friends are a good support system after you've become a bit less emotional and a bit more reason. And don't argue with them about it, there's no argument to be had. Let them be supportive, don't plead your case. The case is closed.

Steady on, as they say in Great Britain. You may still be a bit depressed about it, but don't carry it around, don't wear your heart on your sleeve. You'll soon become a drag, and your friends may rightfully begin to avoid you (not without reason). When you change your behavior and change your language, then your feelings and perspective can change.

Do not contact your ex or any of their friends. Maintain that space at this time.

Don't wallow in your sadness too long, but don't rush into dating either. Rebound dating isn't really good for anyone and never lasts. It may even be cruel to the rebound, giving them false hope for a reliable relationship of their own with you. It's about knowing just what your needs and wants are, what their value is, and how you can get them.

If you'd hoped to be friends with your ex, wait as long as you reasonably can. Seeing them may easily cause a backslide into emotionally vulnerable territory. You want to be as strong as you can as an individual, or perhaps in a new relationship, before you revisit the old. Especially in the later case, as it could bring up feelings of jealousy and mistrust in your new relationship, and it could emotionally derail you and ruin a good, new romance.

But is it wise to stay friends? It's a nice idea to stay friends with your ex, and that surely is possible. But to call it tricky is an understatement.

Before you even think about being friends, the question comes to when it's safe to do so. Has it been long enough? I said this before but it's worth repeating. Stay away from your ex for a significant stretch of time. Come back too soon you never really got out at all.

Some people follow the *fifty-percent equation*, which states that you'll mourn a relationship for half the length of its total duration. If it was a six-year affair, you may spend as long as three years recovering from it.

Yikes! That's a lot of time.

But there's more to the decision than time. How difficult was it to move on after the breakup? Do you think you're strong enough to resist it or to go through it again? Have you really learned your lessons and advanced since the breakup? Are you ready to bring more to the relationship than you did before? Are you ready to correct whatever it was you did wrong before?

Because the initial risk of doing this is that you'll have to resist that old attraction. If your partner still does not, you're in for more pain. And though that may change, one of you would have to change significantly first.

There's also the chance of a possible mutual attraction. Unless what you want is to reignite the partnership, you don't want to sleep together at this point anymore than you do just after the breakup. It's likely to cause all manner of backsliding, overthinking, negative self-talk, doubt, presumption, assumption, false hope, and emotional complications. If you can resist it, do.

To be a friend of your ex is going to require that you change your perspective. You have to visualize, to externalize the person (your ex) from the problem (the breakup and ensuing separation). And you won't be able to act with them as if they were still your partner, no touching or flirting or presumptions of any kind. That means you'll have to find another way to deal with this person, one which is friendly despite the five-hundred-pound gorilla in the room.

If you're collected, calm, friendly, and funny, you'll be fine. Lean on your strengths and keep your distance. If anything, that will inspire admiration for your composure, and it will do wonders for your confidence.

If you're going to stay friends with your ex, make sure you always handle yourself with grace and cool. Never, never lose your cool with snotty remark, eye-rolls, huffs or sighs or other passive/aggressive displays. Your friendship won't last long, and you'll be letting your ex (and everybody else) know that a healthy friendship isn't what you really want and probably isn't really possible.

You may have grown up together. In that case, your time as a couple the first time wasn't necessarily the beginning and end of your relationship, just a significant chapter. But there was a significant chapter before it and could well be another significant chapter after it. You were friends first, and that could yet be the case again. In this case, and in others, you may succeed in becoming friends again, the friends you were before your love or the friend you were before your breakup. Those things are likely to survive, even if the romance did not.

You may even find you have a stronger friendship than before, a new and more mature friendship because you are new and more mature people.

OTHER WAYS OF COPING WITH A BREAKUP

The main thing about dealing with a breakup is communication; sharing just enough with your friends for a sounding board without becoming a pain or a sourpuss about it. Go to therapy if you need to, but first practice positive self-thought, keep a growth-oriented mindset, externalize the events from the person. Concentrate on the good and how to make things better. Set some goals and achieve them according to a timeline, with smaller goals set out in advance. Refocus on creative or productive things instead of self-pity or overthinking, which are counter-productive.

Keep yourself healthy with a good diet, limited alcohol, and physical exercise. Join a workout or self-defense course (or go back to the one you quit after three weeks when you were a couple), read a book or join a book club. Host couples' game night even if you're not in a couple, because this way you can be the gamemaster! Hey, it's *something*.

You might rethink some more personal activities, like journaling or writing a short story or novel. Chronicling your relationship could make a great story and help you work out any lingering feelings you may have. It's a tremendously cathartic exercise and you just may come up with a great novel or screenplay.

Purge everything of theirs from your life. No love letters, no pictures. It's more than just symbolic, it's important to convince yourself that you're not holding onto the past.

Make a list of your positive qualities. These are the easiest things to lose sight of but the most important things to remember. After being rejected, you may feel worthless and incapable. Take the physical steps to remind yourself that this isn't true. Keep the list where you can see it. Make copies and put it in a variety of places if you need to.

Go to three new places; drives into neighborhoods you've never seen, a city park you've never been to, a restaurant you've never tried. Avoid the places you used to go together; they'll only obstruct your progress.

Make a list of your partner's negative qualities. After your own positive qualities, these are the first things you forget but the most important to keep in mind. It's easy to remember the good stuff, but it was the bad stuff which ended the relationship, right? So, they were even more important then, apparently, and they could be of ultimate importance now.

Purge your social media life of your partner's friends, family, groups which you might have shared, your partner especially. Do not follow them on Facebook or go to their websites. Don't cyberstalk them, don't chat in IM.

It sounds counterintuitive, but you should let go of the idea of closure. Nobody really gets that. If you can't get over it on your own, no final talk will really do anything. It may even open old wounds or prevent new wounds from healing. Also, closure just isn't natural. It'd be great if we had it all the time, and we're trained to anticipate and desire it (everything from graduation to retirements to funerals are designed to give us this feeling). But graduation only begins other adventures, other studies and other, higher degrees of accomplishment. A lot of people go on to keep learning their entire lives. There's no real closure for them and that's fine. In fact, closure can be accepted by the growth-minded person who refuses perfectionism. It's the overthinking, negative self-talking perfectionist who can't get over a lack of closure, and that in itself is a lack of closure. Even if you get your closure talk, you're just as likely to feel unsatisfied, to overthink until you think of something else you could have said or would still like to say. Closure is a lost cause and a fool's errand.

If you're a spiritual person, this is the time to cling to that. There's great wisdom about love and relationships and faith and hope and doubt in all the great traditions. Be openhearted and open-minded and you may surprised at what you find there. This is also a good time for community, for some shared strength. And it'll give you something else to think about for a few hours a week, remind you that your problems are small in comparison, that you're part of something bigger, more powerful, more positive.

FINDING A NEW RELATIONSHIP

Assuming you don't want to go back but you do want to go forward, it's time to start looking for a new relationship. The *where's* and the *hows* of this are already pretty well covered in other sections of this book. Favored personal activities, workshops and workouts, lessons and classes; churches and volunteer organizations are all good places to meet new people. Friends and coworkers may have people they can set you up with. But be careful of this, as a fractious romance could divide loyalties and destroy friendships as well as romances.

And there's the internet, of course. It's chock-a-block with dating sites of every sort, chat lines and Facebook groups and clubs. Naturally you'll want to be very cautious about people you meet online. The extent of criminal activity there is beyond the imaginings of good-hearted people, who are exactly their prey of choice; lonely, heart-broken people especially. Guard your personal information, never give out your home address or phone number, request multiple photographs or a personal photo to prove you're not being catfished.

You can always arrange to meet somewhere for coffee.

No matter where you go to meet someone, a bar or a resort or our only moon Luna, it's going to come back to what you're communicating, to others and to yourself.

First of all, look to within. Whatever you need to truly make you happy has to reside inside yourself. You have to make yourself happy before you can make anyone else happy. If you're miserable, nobody can be happy for you. So, ask yourself what you want or need, visualize and actualize. Nobody can make you complete, and you can't do that for anyone else. You can only create a more complete relationship.

Live your life the way you want to. Then you'll find and attract someone who wants to live as you do, instead of somebody whose lifestyle preferences are wildly divergent to your own. You don't want to get caught up in the, *I love you, you're perfect, now change* syndrome!

If you're going to learn new things and expand your horizons that way, think about choosing those things which the people you're fond of or attracted to do. Does a person you like bowl? Learn how, it's not that hard; few things are. Along these lines, if you see qualities in others which you admire, adopt those qualities for yourself. Emulation is the way people learn from early childhood on. If somebody has a certain quality you admire, be it humor, quiet, boldness, reason, make it your own. Nobody owns these things!

Get back to the meaningful things in life. Bond with friends, reread your childhood journals, take long walks outside. Reconnect to the natural world and that will help you reconnect to yourself.

Take it slow when you do meet someone new. There's no rush. We've already seen the problems that can cause. There's no need to use a fixed mindset to presume how the relationship will go. You'll never overthink it forward, only backward. If anything, you might think about *under*thinking it. Don't assume control, but also don't be negligent. Just realize some things aren't entirely in your control, no matter how they turn out.

When you meet someone, you have a good connection with, allow that connection to develop and grow. If the person is a soul mate, he or she will also be into you, so if you both pay genuine attention to each other then something will develop.

COMMUNICATING IN A NEW RELATIONSHIP

You've been through a healthy period of grieving; you've engaged in some new or favored activities which get you out of the house. You're still wrestling with some lingering feelings, but that's okay. They'll fade with time, you're pretty sure about that. You're ready.

You've been sizing up prospective new partners and you've found one. He or she seems interested in you too, in fact they've made it clear. Now it's time to start dating again.

But keep two things in mind. On one hand, you probably haven't been on a first date or in a courtship scenario for a long time. You may not have been that great at it to begin with (some people are awkward in this stage). And you've been enduring a lot of other things, so you may well be a bit rusty at those awkward first few exchanges.

They're also crucial exchanges, ones which will set the tone for the entire relationship, if there is going to be one.

You're also coming off a breakup, so you're not exactly a blank slate. So, lets take a look at some crucial *dos* and *don'ts* of getting things off on a good foot!

First of all, do not mention your ex, not once. Don't mention any of your exes, in fact. This new person assumes you've had other partners, and hearing about them can be insulting to them, as if you'd rather be with any of them. It also sounds like you're bragging about how many partners you've had. And if you keep referencing your last partner, who broke up with you, that's a whole other sad sac of potatoes. It indicates that you're not really over it, and you're probably not. It's very offensive to compare a new date to an old partner, as the old has so much advantage over the new. It's certainly not flattering, and that's what the first few exchanges are for.

Speaking of flattery, don't let that be a one-way street. Women may be used to being flattered, but they often neglect to return the compliment. Men like and need to hear that too, and it's just selfish or thoughtless to neglect it to others. If you want a man with confidence, make him feel confident. And you're a hypocrite if you get snitty when you're not complimented if you don't share the compliments yourself.

Naturally, you'll want to stick to the standards. Don't lie, don't interrupt, listen actively, engage in eye contact with discretion. Ask them about themselves, direct attention away from yourself. Be graceful and generous in your rhetoric about others.

Don't rush things. Don't be too eager to create a life's love. If that's going to happen, it's going to happen. So, no early references to family, children, love, marriage.

Don't go too deep too soon. No confessions of past traumas on the first date. In time, but not on the first date. No emotional breakdowns. Don't be clingy. Be comfortable with yourself, live the life you want, have integrity. These things will serve you in every situation, but especially when you're making those crucial first impressions.

14

THE HOWS, WHEN, AND WHYS OF GETTING BACK TOGETHER

REUNITED AND IT FEELS SO GOOD ...?

Breakups can be rough, but they can also be handled so that things remain civil and neither party suffered needlessly. Time has gone by and you've moved on. Maybe you've had another relationship or two. You've come to grips with your feelings for your ex, you've externalized the events of your breakup and of your relationship from yourselves as individuals. And you've learned from your mistakes, become a better person for it. You've come to grips and any anger or hurt you may have had over the breakup and events leading up to it, and you have fond memories of your ex and the better times you shared.

You may even have managed to strike up a post-breakup friendship, reconnecting on some level, and that's gratifying. The parts of your friendship that were strong before and during have proven to endure, and maybe they're stronger now than ever. Or you may have made a clean break of it, for the mutual best.

But it's also possible that you retain feelings for your ex, that the notion of getting back together lingers in the back of your brain and your heart. It's not just the occasional flash, but something that keeps coming back to you.

Is it possible that you could get back with your ex? Should you? When will you know it's the right move, and how do you communicate your way through getting back together? Let's take a deeper look, beginning with when to know if getting back together is the right move.

THE FOUR RS AND THE FIVE STAGES OF REUNION

But first, it's important to note that any reunion, no matter how, when, or why it happens, is predicated on certain things, handily known as the *Four Rs.*

The four Rs, by the way, apply to both parties, no matter who broke up with who or who is coming back to who. Everybody has their portions of the Four Rs to shoulder in a situation like this.

First, there must be *remorse*. An apology, no matter how sincere, isn't going to do it. The cycle of abuse is furthered by it's fourth stage, contrition. What is required is legitimate remorse, a desire not only to correct the ill feelings but to change or eradicate the behavior which created the ill feelings to begin with. This must be more than proclaimed, it has to be evinced. It has to be honest. They have to express an understanding of your pain, and of their part in causing that pain.

There must also be *responsibility*. Real remorse requires responsibility. If you transgressed, it's not enough just to show remorse because you feel responsible, you must be responsible for your future actions. You must take responsibility and act responsibly. Don't repeat those old mistakes, don't fall back into those old patterns.

You have to demonstrate *recognition* of the other person's feelings, through calm and clear communication which avoids shaming and blaming.

And last, there must be some remedy. Making amends is one thing, but taking up a plan of action is the best way to make sure all that remorse, responsibility, and recognition goes to positive, constructive use. That could mean therapy, or just a commitment to certain techniques in this book. They're designed to keep things running smoothly and preventing communication breakdown and crises, the root of almost every relationship failure as we have seen.

Remorse, responsibility, recognition, and remedy.

There are also the Five Stages of Reunion. If you're going to get back with your ex, you must have a working knowledge of these five stages.

The first is the fantasy stage. At least one partner has likely been thinking about this reunion, fantasizing about it perhaps for years. They've visualized it, planned it, overthought it. This is the first stage of any reunion, the desire which ignites the reunion. Granted, there could be times when the ex-partners bump into each other completely by happenstance, both perfectly at peace with life yet who happen to be single and they fall back in together.

Could be.

The second stage is the re-introduction. Seeing each other on the subway or on Facebook, this spark hits the powder keg of fantasy, and a reunion may begin. Of course, it could be that you've been a coworker with your ex during the entire span between the breakup and the reunion, and you've gone through all the necessary healing steps in spite of that.

Could be.

The so-called morning after is the period after the great thrush of the re-introduction. Something's either going to happen then or not at all. This is where the real work starts and the real fun too.

You may enter a limbo stage, where trepidations arise and one partner withdraws. It's natural, and it can be dealt with if it's understood for what it is.

The fifth stage is resolution. Whatever the doubts of the limbo stage, the work of the morning after stage will help determine how things are resolved. This is the proof in the pudding, as they say.

So, realize when you are reuniting that you may be in a limbo stage, but that does not mean the resolution will go one way or the other. Be mindful that the re-introduction phase is thrilling but brief and that the morning after stage is enduring.

Now, let's move ahead and take a closer look at why you'd want to go back to your ex even after having failed with them before.

WHY GO BACK?

Make sure you're doing it for the right reasons. Are you truly longing for that ex, or are you simply lonely? Are you feeling old and lazy and sick of telling your life story to somebody new? Are you feeling like you're not getting any younger and it's time to settle for whatever you can get? You'll know if these are good motivators or not, and what your true motives are, once you employ some of the techniques in this book. Make a list of reasons to go back and reasons to stay away, prioritize the items on each list. The numbers will help you figure it out (numbers don't lie... sort of).

Ask yourself what advice you'd give to your best friend. Ask your imaginary friend why they want to go back. Challenge them. You'll be getting to your true motivations, wants and desires. Exercise the *5 Whys* technique to discover if your motives are positive or if you're acting out of some misguided instinct.

WHEN YOU GROW BACK, YOU GOT TO GO BACK

In terms of getting back together, the *when* of it is crucial. You can't go back if you haven't been gone, right? You have to make sure that the issues have been dealt with, your issues anyway, since they're the only ones you can truly control. You have to know you've moved on. How long is that? At what point do you know you've made it over the bridge to the other side? It's going to be different for everybody. But here are a few things to consider.

It could be that the answer is never. It's pretty reasonable to think about getting back together, simply as a result of having gotten over a person. You can see the mistakes you made, the good and the bad of the relationship, the true qualities of your ex as a partner and as a friend. If you've made peace and abandoned the rancid emotional residue of the experience. And there had been a real chemistry there at one point, something most people long for, something that's increasingly hard to find, especially as one gets older and more particular in their habits and perspectives. So, it's pretty natural to be attracted to the idea of the relationship at its best, and to be convinced that it's within reach. That's the way human beings are, we're trained to try to achieve the things we imagine. And it's always possible and sometimes a positive thing.

Sometimes not.

So, make sure in your case whether you're just being nostalgic or unrealistic. Lot's of things seem like a good idea, but make sure this is really one of them.

Experts will tell you that the only time to get back together is if the issues which ended the relationship have been resolved. And that only makes good sense. It doesn't matter how much your perspective has changed if the behaviors haven't changed. Remember, whatever broke you up before is going to happen again … unless those problems have been resolved.

And perhaps they have. These issues came up between the two individuals, but they were born from the behavior of each individual first, then in combination. So, if each individual has taken time in the post-breakup period to get back in touch with themselves, remained growth-minded, and bettered themselves, the recoupling could succeed. But the odds are against it, and it's tricky for a number of reasons.

Check these factors when the idea of getting back together pops up over and over again.

Make sure you've taken enough time to grieve. You have to process those emotions; you have to clear the residue from your system. If you're going back, you have to go back clean if you want your new relationship to be healthy. But if you've come through the grieving process and your longing endures, you might consider any possibilities which come along. Make sure there is a possibility first though, or you'll languish in that romantic limbo of longing.

Make sure you've identified your need or want and prioritize. Ask yourself some if/then questions about getting back together, visualize it. Be practical. Though they remain dear to you, were the issues you had simply matters of incompatibility? Your ex is not likely to have changed their core values or world view, and they're probably never going to; nor will you. It's possible, and it does happen, but it happens less and less as we get older (unless you're Ebenezer Scrooge).

Was this a toxic relationship? Was one partner abusive? If so, those things aren't likely to have changed, and it's just not a matter of when.

They never will change, so the answer to the question when must be never.

But if the relationship had been good for you and maybe you were the toxic element and you've learned from that and changed your ways, and your ex is still interested, it's in the realm of possibility. Make sure you really have changed and that you won't backslide into old behaviors. Some people may trigger that, and it's likely that your ex was one of them. You'd best have self-control and know how to deal with those triggers.

Strangely, some people long for exes who treated them poorly or abusively. They crave the contrition which follows the abuse, perhaps. They may have a martyr complex or a victim complex which require abuse. These conditions need serious therapy, however, and that should be engaged and the issue resolved before any serious connections can be made or healthy relationship created.

Has your ex told you that they want to get back together? That's pretty key. Everything we've just been over is predicated on the fact your ex does want you back. Even if you're friends (especially if you are) it's foolish to start planning a reunion unless you know for sure it's what your ex wants. The only way to know that is if they say it. Do not presume or assume in this case, mistaking the post-breakup friendship for more than that.

Only consider getting back together if you're sure that you both want the same thing. This is no time to go into things with different goals. If one still wants kids and the other still doesn't, that's still going to be a dealbreaker.

A word on having kids. Children are not things to be used as barter in romantic negotiations. You want to be back with your ex, but your ex wants a child; so, you decide to give her a child in exchange for a balm for your desire. That is not a reason to have a child, for so many obvious reasons.

It may not work, first of all, and then you're stuck with an ex and a child you have to pay for. I don't mean to be cold, but that ain't cheap. Do a few if/then questions to visualize what this could all look like; it's not a pretty picture. Then you may come to resent your child, which you never really wanted, and you may become psychologically abusive, or abusive in other ways. Your child may come to resent you, residual feelings from your ex. Custody battles are brutal on everyone involved.

And having children is one of the most challenging things a person can do. It brings all kinds of pressures and difficulties. Parenting has been known to destroy marriages on its own, never mind keeping them together.

Only have children if that's what you both truly want, then make sure you can pull it off comfortably. But that's another subject for another book.

Before you get back together, ask yourself how many times you broke up the first time. A lot of relationships don't simply end, as we've seen. People take breaks, or they reconsider and quickly come back. And this pattern can repeat several times before a (presumably) final break. If that was the case with this pairing, it's likely to happen again. Do you really want a relationship which is little more than a series of breakups? How likely is it that this won't be the case again? What's changed specifically to insure it won't happen again?

Have you both resolved your individual issues? If not, they'll come up again.

But if it's what both you and your ex want, and you feel the timing is right, the next thing to consider is how to do it correctly.

HOW TO COMMUNICATE THROUGH A REUNION

You and your ex have decided to give it another go. This time, you're determined to make it work. Great. But it's a difficult and treacherous time for both parties, and care must be taken when communicating through a reunion.

If you're going to begin these negotiations, and that's what they are, do it someplace casual. Unlike a breakup, this is something you can do in a café or favorite restaurant. Nobody's likely to throw a fit during this conversation.

This conversation more than most requires you use a lot of the same tactics you used when communicating through a communication breakdown.

- Be empathetic.
- Be Honest.
- Address behavior, not character.
- If you must address your partner's behavior, follow it up

quickly with a solution, which you should already have prepared in advance.
- When you move from questions to declarations, keep them about yourself.
- Avoid triggers and triggered responses and be prepared to walk away if you have to.
- When you *are* speaking, however, use collaborative language like *we, our, us.*
- Think before you speak.
- Be sober. Be kind; no personal insults. Be brief and don't repeat yourself.
- Be conscious of your body language, don't be aggressive with your gestures.
- Be diplomatic.
- Think good thoughts.
- Don't be afraid to apologize. It doesn't cost you anything, and it's probably pretty reasonable that you should.

In greater particular:

Keep it light, focus on the good memories before you move on to confronting the issues, which you'll have to do. But don't get bogged down in that, and start off on a strongly positive note.

When you're making it official and negotiating your recoupling, make sure you address old issues. Put them to bed once and for all or they will creep up and be problematic, probably sooner rather than later.

Make sure trust is secured. Clear communication can only happen when trust is strong. In fact, without trust there is no relationship to communicate about. If there were trust issues before, and that's likely after a breakup, this has to be externalized and discussed. It should be separated from the people, as in narrative therapy, and then settled. It must be agreed that trust must be established and respected, or there's little reason to move forward.

Along those lines, make sure you've truly forgiven this person for whatever's happened. If you're still carrying around emotional baggage over past events, they'll only come up again and probably recur. It also means you haven't truly gotten over it, that you're still healing. That means you haven't really reached self-actualization and you're not ready to rejoin that coupling.

As you should always do but especially during a recoupling is collect your thoughts before you raise any issues. This is a careful negotiation, after all, it requires diplomacy. Don't just wing it or you might blow it.

Share your experiences from when you were apart. You don't want any secrets at this stage in the game. And what you've done and learned surely has made you the qualified person to rejoin that relationship. Any partner would be interested in hearing about that. It may even be necessary to help instill trust and put away the old hurts, proof that you really have changed.

In general, take things slow. Moving too quickly might have been the thing which drove you apart in the first place. Let your partner be the more-excited of the two. And though you'll be excited at the notion of reuniting, there's no reason to rush. You've waited this long, and if the reunion is real it's going to last. Don't rush this.

Try seeing it as a new chapter, not a new relationship. Because that's what it is, and only when you're being realistic about who you are, who your partner is, and what you're doing, will you be able to create the relationship you could have had all along.

Make sure you're seeing things clearly, not through rose-colored glasses. That may have been fine when you were first falling in love, but you have to be clear-eyed and reasonable this time. No more unrealistic expectations which lead to disappointment, right? Right.

Know that you might not have everybody's support. Your family and friends are apt to be skeptical. But don't let them sway you if this is really what you and your ex want. It's your relationship, not theirs. But don't let it alienate you from them either. Reassure them that you appreciate their support but that you've resolved the things which could be and needed to be resolved.

Remember that you're not with a different person. This is essentially the same person you knew before. They may have improved or evolved, or your expectations may have changed, but you have to know who you're dealing with and how to deal with that person. Remember what you've learned about them and about yourself, and remember what you've learned from this book and keep those lessons in mind. Use the techniques to keep the communication open and healthy, or things are likely to go sour again.

WHEN A REUNION DOESN'T WORK OUT

You finally returned to your life's love, worked out all the issues, even employed a lot of the tips and tricks in this book to get and stay closer.

But it still isn't working out. Your friends are shaking their heads, *I-told-you-so* expressions on their faces. You may even feel foolish about undertaking such a thing, like a failure. And to a degree those things may even be true.

But the important thing, as always, is that you avoid negative self-talk. Separate your worth as an individual from the worth of the couple. Sometimes two people just aren't going to make it together, despite everybody's best efforts and intentions. There are some common reasons for that, and they should be familiar by now.

Keeping secrets is a big reason these reunions fail. Things did happen in the interval, and withholding them only creates suspicion, doubt, a downward spiral which is often fatal to a romantic reunion. Likewise, lying about what had happened or with who is a terrible idea. Lying is the opposite of clear communication, and clear communication is key to a successful relationship at any stage, this stage in particular, when guards are likely to be up.

Pushing things too hard or too fast is another big mistake. Sadly, most of these people haven't read this book! But you have and you know better. In this case, a romantic reunion is a big move and your partner may have trepidations. Rushing things only bears them out.

Ignoring the stages of reunion is a crucial mistake. Know them, discuss them, digest them, know where you are and what's coming up ahead.

Being insensitive to the changes in and feelings of the other person will kill a relationship at any stage, a reunion in particular. Lack of sensitivity is likely at the heart of the original breakup.

Ignoring the past is another reason reunions fail. People forget the lessons learned and backslide into their old habits.

Disrespect is also inappropriate, personally or of the partner's other bonds outside the relationship. This is no time to be a splitter. Those people may have been the support group who got your partner through the first breakup, their place in your partner's life need to be respected, and so do they.

Because people change over time, it could be that one person changed in ways the other simply doesn't like. Drastic lifestyle choices like veganism, for example, or radical religious conversion. People change, but not always to your taste; and the same goes for you.

It can also be that the old wounds keep opening up, that they'll never truly heal in the presence of the other. If this is the sad case, both parties should be able to recognize it. It's a sad truth that things cannot be unsaid or unheard, we can't turn back the clock. And nobody is doing anybody any good at all in refusing to face the facts.

If it works out the second time, that's great. If it doesn't, at least you gave it a good try and you'll be able to move forward certain that it just wasn't meant to be. Keep searching and you'll find what and who you're looking for. And when you find that person, you'll know just how to secure a healthier relationship through clear communication!

CONCLUSION

Well, it's been quite a trip! We've worked though the *how, why, where, and when* and *who* of beginning a relationship, helping it to flourish, avoiding its pitfalls. We've looked at different ways of getting through a breakup, of healing and growing, and even reuniting with that partner.

We've looked at your own deepest wants and needs and motivations, ways you might think and ways you might change your thinking. These truly are things you can take out of the realm of romance or intimacy and into the rest of your life. We've touched briefly on spirituality and meditation, and we can only recommend you go on to research those things further. We don't promote any in particular, but they can work in various combinations, like most of the things in this book. You'll be assembling a new library of skills and techniques to make your interactions go more smoothly and reduce conflict in every area of your life.

You've picked up a virtual education in psychology, hopefully having learned more about yourself and the world around you. That's the nature of a heathy psyche and a happy life.

No matter where you are in the romantic cycle, you've got the tools you need to put things right and make things better, to know when to walk away and when to come back.

Use this information in every corner and on every level of your relationship, and your life. You can do what seemed impossible, and you can help others do it too. And keep working. Don't resist the idea of coming back later and rereading this book. Unless you've used every technique, there are bound to be more things here you haven't tried, things you missed the first time. Think of this book and others like it as a reference manual, to be referred to whenever you need. There may be other facets of your life that could use improvement, or the lives of those you love. Keep reading, keep growing, keep learning, and keep living. Stay openhearted and open-minded. Stay healthy and be happy!